THE POLITICS OF ZONING

NUMBER FOUR
METROPOLITAN POLITICS SERIES

THE POLITICS OF
ZONING

THE NEW YORK EXPERIENCE

S. J. MAKIELSKI, Jr.

COLUMBIA UNIVERSITY PRESS

New York and London 1966

S. J. Makielski, Jr., is Assistant Professor of Government
at the University of Virginia.

To S. K. M.

ACKNOWLEDGMENTS

Although it is not possible to mention all those who have contributed to making this study possible, I would like to express a special debt of gratitude to Professor Wallace S. Sayre of Columbia University. His patience as teacher and gentleness as critic saw this study through many drafts and rescued it from many mistakes.

Professor David B. Truman also made an immeasurable contribution in ideas and concepts. The Metropolitan Region Program of Columbia University and the Ford Foundation provided the essential ways and means for my graduate education and for this book.

The many others who through their knowledge of and participation in the politics of zoning made the study possible must go without being thanked by name. They were the actors about whom this book is written. They gave their time to answer my questions and to volunteer their knowledge. Without them and their frankness there would be no book. But their battles are not over; to mention them by name would be ungrateful since most still have future decisions to make and future commitments to fulfill.

Needless to say, any errors that remain are mine and are in no way the fault of those who have contributed to this study.

April, 1965   S. J. MAKIELSKI, JR.

CONTENTS

TABLES

METROPOLITAN POLITICS SERIES

This is the fourth in a series of books resulting from the metropolitan study program begun at Columbia University in 1957 and supported by a grant from the Ford Foundation.

The faculty committee supervising this program and serving as editors of the series are Wallace S. Sayre, Chairman, Richard E. Neustadt and David B. Truman of the Department of Public Law and Government of Columbia University, and William N. Cassella, Jr., of the National Municipal League.

ABBREVIATIONS
OF AGENCIES AND ORGANIZATIONS

AIA	American Institute of Architects
BSA	Board of Standards and Appeals
CMZ	Citizens Committee for Modern Zoning
CPC	City Planning Commission
CZC	Citizens Zoning Committee
HB&A	Harrison, Ballard, and Allen
MREBA	Metropolitan Real Estate Boards Association
VWS&S	Voorhees, Walker, Smith, and Smith

INTRODUCTION

This is a study of urban politics. It is the study of how public policy is made in one city and how that public policy came into being. While no single case study can hope to describe all aspects of the complex phenomenon that is political behavior in a large city, this book attempts to outline and analyze a policy-making process that is characteristic of New York City and to answer the questions: What are the major features of the process? How does it work? And what does it do?

The Problem

Land use zoning—the control of privately owned real estate by public policy—came into official being in New York City in 1916. Since that time it has become one of the most extensively used means of controlling the urban environment in the nation.[1] Zoning is used—so the zoning ordinances say—to promote the "health, safety, and welfare" of the inhabitants of urban areas. It is also used to encourage the city's economy, to protect social values, and (hopefully) to bring some degree of order and rationality to the present and future development of the city.

Zoning is almost entirely associated with urban areas. Although an increasing number of municipal functions are being tied to the policy processes of higher governmental levels—highway construction, urban renewal, education, and taxation, to name a few—zoning has been and remains the province of local government. Because zoning touches the lives and activities of many who live and work in cities, and because it is a policy area that is pursued by municipal governments, the study of zoning provides the opportunity to watch an urban political system in action in a "pure" form.

The study of zoning as public policy has further importance, however. Those who have been the proponents of zoning have been so in the hope of resolving some of the problems of urbanization. In this context, zoning has long been associated with the municipal reform movement—a movement whose members have attempted to "do something" about cities. The history of zoning in New York City is also a modest history of the city's reform movement.

The municipal reformers, however, are only part of the galaxy of actors who appear in the zoning policy-making system. To understand the role of municipal reform in the politics of zoning, it is necesary to examine and understand the governmental, economic, and social interests that are also represented. These interests, separately and collectively, have helped to shape the policies that have emerged in zoning and city planning in New York.

Traditionally, zoning has been studied from either a legal view or a prescriptive approach. The legal view has focused almost entirely on the examination and interpretation of court decisions in zoning law.[2] The prescriptive approach has concentrated on comparing existing zoning laws or designing and recommending provisions to conform with the stated or implicit goals of the city planning movement.[3] Those approaching zoning from the prescriptive viewpoint have hoped to improve the writing and application of zoning laws and thereby to help meet the problems of urbanization.

These two approaches provide invaluable raw materials for those who are engaged in the ongoing battles of municipal land policy and city planning. Although this study proposes to break with both traditions, it is not intended as a slight to the basic utility of either older approach. It simply suggests that there is more to the story. An understanding of how policy is arrived at will help to make both the legal interpretation of zoning law and the design of better ordinances a more meaningful task.

A further purpose is intended, however. I hope to show that the examination of a policy area, particularly one that encompasses the major interests of a great city, can be used as a means for better understanding cities and what happens in them. To do this, I propose to examine how policy decisions in zoning are made by tracing the major events in the history of zoning in New York City, by discovering and analyzing the actors who participated in these events and what roles they played, and then by attempting to relate participant and process.

Design of the Study

This study examines the history of zoning in New York City from 1910 to 1960, concentrating, in the main, on those zoning proposals and efforts that were "comprehensive"—that is, that attempted to zone the entire city instead of having application to only limited parts of the city. The efforts comprehensively to zone the city have been the major innovative efforts, and they have evoked the greatest response. They most vividly show the city's political system in operation.

In addition, however, some attention will be given to the quieter struggles around the less-than-comprehensive zoning efforts, since these struggles help to illuminate the underlying structure of the policy-making process. While this study is by no means a complete history of zoning in New York City, it is aimed at presenting the major patterns and characteristics of the zoning system in that city.

Two major assumptions have governed the approach of the study. The first has been that zoning may be profitably studied by relying on the viewpoints and methods of political science. The data were examined with the purpose of revealing the relation of governmental agencies, nongovernmental actors, and the patterns of behavior that link these participants. This assumption must limit the scope of the endeavor. At no point has an effort been made to evaluate the outcomes of political processes in terms of whether these outcomes are "good" or "bad"—desirable or undesirable. The question asked was not: What should have happened? It was: What did happen?

The second major assumption is that zoning in New York City can be viewed as a *system*. There are few more confusing or more complicated terms in political science than "system," but for the purposes of this study the *zoning system* simply refers to those behavior patterns and actors which have been associated with each other because of their tie to zoning as public policy.[4]

In general, the sources relied upon for the study were the familiar ones for political science research. The files of New York City newspapers, the reports and records of governmental agencies and nongovernmental interest groups, and direct personal interviews all were used.

PART ONE

ZONING
IN NEW YORK CITY

I

THE RESOLUTION
OF 1916

New York City's Zoning Resolution of 1916 was a major innovation in municipal public policy. It was the product of
municipal reform, a set of responses to complex economic and
social problems, and the claims of local and special interests.

1897–1910: Politics, Problems, and Reformers

REFORM AND FUSION. "Greater New York City" was born in
a welter of political maneuver and strife. After years of agitation, the five boroughs (or counties) of Manhattan, the Bronx,
Brooklyn, Queens, and Staten Island were "consolidated" into
one city, effective January 1, 1898.[1] The first three years of
the new city's life saw a bitter contest for control of the city's
governmental and political structure. On one side of the contest there was a strong thrust for centralization of the city's
government; on the other, an effort to maintain a maximum
degree of autonomy in the five boroughs.[2] The outcome, ratified by the City Charter of 1901, tended to favor the proponents
of borough autonomy.

The Charter of 1901 established a bicameral legislative body:
the Board of Estimate and Apportionment and the Board of
Aldermen. The Board of Estimate, however, was by far the
more powerful of the two bodies and increased in influence
with the passage of time. The Board of Estimate represented
a compromise between the ideas of centralized city government

and borough autonomy: three members—the mayor, the comptroller, and the president of the Board of Aldermen—were
elected "city-wide." The remaining members were the elected
presidents of each of the five boroughs.[3]

Party control gravitated to the "Regular" Democratic "machines" in the boroughs, with Tammany Hall (the Manhattan
Democratic organization) having the upper hand. The Democratic Regulars, with firm roots in the county and borough
party organizations, controlled the city's governmental machinery. They were, however, consistently faced with a threat
from the local Republicans. Although the Republicans were
a chronic minority party, they persistently searched for weaknesses in the Democratic ranks.

There was, further, a third and significant force in the political life of the city: the municipal reformers.

Although municipal reform (hereafter referred to as Reform) was not new to the city, in the years immediately preceding and following the turn of the century the Reformers
established firm organizational roots through such groups as
the Citizens Union and the City Club. They attracted businessmen, professional people, and the civic-minded, whatever their
nominal party allegiance.[4]

The Reform persuasion was a product of impatience with
the "corruption" and the "inefficiency" of machine politics.
The Reform credo argued for "rational, efficient," and business-like approaches to local government. The Reformer favored nonpartisan elections, civil service reform, city planning,
and "good government" in general.[5] He felt the city should
be approached from a "general, community-wide" view.[6]

The principal weakness of Reform in New York City lay
in its inability to put its program into effect. Although the Citizens Union created grass-roots organizations in the hope of winning office, it was not until the Reformers and the Republicans
allied in 1901 that both found a way to defeat the Regular

Democrats. Thus, "Fusion"—the political marriage of the Reformers and the Regular Republicans—came into being.

The Fusionists won the mayoralty in 1901 but two years later the alliance fell apart, and the Regular Democrats won in 1903 and again in 1905.[7]

In 1909, although the Democratic nominee, William J. Gaynor, won the office of mayor, the Fusionists were able to elect two Reformers: George McAneny as borough president of Manhattan and John Purroy Mitchel as president of the Board of Aldermen.

Fusion thus not only provided a means by which Reformers and Republicans could defeat the Regular Democrats at the polls, it also placed Reformers in positions where they could influence municipal policy-making.

REFORMERS AND PROBLEMS. Many of the Reform-oriented turned their attention to electoral reforms, to civil service reform, or to the problems of the city's fiscal affairs. A handful, however, were profoundly concerned with the direction of the city's physical development.

George McAneny and Edward M. Bassett, both Reformers, came to dominate the field of city planning for several decades. McAneny began as a lawyer and a journalist, but was soon drawn into civil service reform.[8] Then for three years (1906 to 1909) he was president of the City Club and was deeply enmeshed in the politics of the city. He successfully stood for the borough presidency of Manhattan in 1909 and was, at the age of forty-one, an admired and skilled politician. He had the Reformer's biases and his experience with the City Club (as president of the City Club he had also been chairman of its Committee on City Planning) had given him a vast and personal knowledge of the city's problems.

Bassett was born in 1863 and spent most of his life in Brooklyn.[9] He was a lawyer, a self-made man, and, like McAneny, had long been in politics. Elected to Congress in

1902 as an "Independent Democrat," he refused to stand for office at the end of his two-year term in the House of Representatives. He found the card-playing, liquor-drinking, hard-living Washingtonians distasteful. In 1907 he was appointed to the Public Service Commission by his former college roommate, the then Governor Charles Evans Hughes, and played an important part in formulating plans for the burgeoning subway system.

Bassett was a Reformer. His interests were primarily in the physical development of the city and he felt more at home with architects and engineers than with his fellow-lawyers. Of an undramatic and economical turn of mind, he was archetypal of the planning ideal: pragmatic, persuasive before an audience, frugal, interested in physical planning, and, paradoxically, a dreamer.

During the years 1907–12, McAneny's and Bassett's interests in subway planning and city planning led them to confer frequently. They, Lawson Purdy (city tax assessor), and Nelson P. Lewis (chief engineer of the Board of Estimate) became close friends and shared a mutual concern in the future of the city.

The future they saw and worried about was a city of buildings of increasing size and height, with the consequence of increased population density.

As Bassett and McAneny saw it, the subways did nothing to relieve the problem of crowding.[10] By encouraging speculation in real estate, by making it possible for greater numbers of people to concentrate near the subway entrances, and by allowing the population to spread into older, settled residential neighborhoods, the subways increased instability and crowding. In Bassett's and McAneny's view, the consequences were appalling: skyscrapers cut off light and air from surrounding buildings; commercial buildings invaded residential areas, and industrial uses invaded both commercial and residential areas; real estate values were forced up to unrealistic levels; and city living became less comfortable, less bearable.[11]

There were, however, no easy solutions to these problems. The laissez-faire tradition was strong: if a man paid money for a piece of land he was entitled to use it as he saw fit. Realtors had been hard hit in a slump triggered by the depression of 1907 and there seemed to be no relief for their plight. They could only cut costs, raise rents and prices, and hope that something might occur to reintroduce stability into the real estate market.[12]

Municipal government had no way of meeting the problems generated by population increases and subway expansion. Although the City Charter gave the Board of Aldermen the power to regulate the heights of tenements,[13] this was a power exercised only lightly by the Tenement House Commission and, further had no application to commercial and industrial uses. Los Angeles, in 1895, and Boston in 1903 had passed very rudimentary laws for controlling building heights and obnoxious uses, but these experiments were still in litigation and were, moreover, of very limited scope.[14] In the years before 1911, further, Bassett and McAneny were immersed in the press of immediate problems and had little time to do more than speculate about the future.

The First Zoning Commission: 1911–1913

The first impetus for building control more extensive than tenement house reform came from the Fifth Avenue Association. This group had a "local" but what seemed to them a dangerously serious problem. The majority of the members of the association were retail garment merchants. Reasonably enough, garment manufacturers located their factories (or rather, their "lofts" where the clothing units were assembled) as near to their principal buyers as possible. This reduced the cost of transportation to the retail outlets for the manufacturers and also simplified dealing with the stores' buying agents. During the noon lunch hour and at closing time, however, times when large numbers of shoppers were in the streets, the loft workers poured onto the already crowded sidewalks—and, in the opinion of the merchants, drove away customers. Further, the wagons and delivery trucks added to congestion in the streets. The Fifth Avenue Association was aware of the prestige problem involved—the mingling of shoppers with workers and of the "best stores" with lofts was distasteful, un-aesthetic, and unconducive to the image that the merchants were attempting to foster. This was expressed by a representative of the association:

Many of them [the lofts] are cheap in construction and appearance and are at the same time of considerable height. . . . These buildings are crowded with their hundreds and thousands of garment workers who swarm down upon the avenue for the lunch hour. . . . They stand upon or move slowly along the sidewalks and choke them up . . . and as work ends at the close of the day, thou-sands of these operators pour out upon the sidewalks within a short space of time, and congest the side streets with a steady stream of humanity that moves its way to the East Side. . . . Shopkeepers complain bitterly of financial loss . . . [because many] women shop-pers tend to avoid the section.[15]

The retail establishments fled uptown along Fifth Avenue in the decade following the turn of the century, seeking less congested, more amenable surroundings. The lofts, in perverse obedience to what seemed to be an inevitable economic logic, followed them. The lofts left behind buildings that were vacant or nearly so, less desirably located, and older. Un-surprisingly, the value of the older buildings dropped radi-cally.[16] By 1911 the area south of Twenty-third Street was in a stage of advanced deterioration, and the area between Twenty-third and Thirty-fourth streets (the new site of most of the major retail stores) was beginning to show signs of in-vasion by the ubiquitous lofts.

The Fifth Avenue Association had been founded in 1907 to meet the loft problem.[17] By 1911 the association had come no nearer to finding a solution. Unable to do anything alone, in 1911 the association's leadership approached George McAneny, Manhattan borough president, with their complaint: congestion, declining land values, declining numbers of shoppers, and no stopping the process. McAneny was deeply involved in the subway system plans, but he listened long enough to create a seven-member, quasi-official Fifth Avenue Commission, all of whom were members of the Fifth Avenue Association except the chief engineer of the Board of Estimate (Nelson P. Lewis). The commission was to consider the problem and write a report that McAneny would sponsor before the Board of Estimate.[18]

Early in March, 1912, the Fifth Avenue Commission reported back to McAneny. As the commission saw it, the only solution to the problem was to limit the heights of buildings in the Fifth Avenue area, an area they defined as running 300 feet both east and west of the avenue. Buildings should be limited to a height of 125 feet, on the theory that this particular height would make loft construction uneconomical without hampering retail activity. The commission included in its report a proposed resolution for McAneny to offer to the Board of Estimate.[19]

The commission had the precedent of the Tenement House Law on its side, although it was arguing for the application of restrictions to a specific geographic area instead of to a class of structures. McAneny was probably aware of the legal problems involved in the difference: tenement regulation could well fall within the "health and welfare" provisions of the state's police powers if attacked in the courts; a geographic districting was not so easily justified and resembled discriminatory (although protective) legislation.[20] McAneny fulfilled his promise, however, and submitted the report to the Board of Estimate on May 9, 1912.[21] Having once introduced the proposal, though, he did not press the issue. The report lay before the board without being brought up for action.

The question lay publicly dormant throughout the summer and early winter of 1912. The Fifth Avenue Association, with an expanding membership, continued to press its cause on McAneny. The president of the association, Robert Grier Cooke, met "frequently" with McAneny and politely requested action.[22]

Meanwhile, McAneny, Bassett, and Lawson Purdy, city tax assessor and a Reformer also, were beginning to contemplate a novel approach to the city's problem. They agreed that one of the basic concerns of the city was building heights and the concomitant loss of light and air, as well as declining land values. The problem did seem to be more acute below Thirty-fourth Street in the Fifth Avenue area, but all three were becoming increasingly aware of broader possibilities. Bassett, in 1911, formed his own Committee on City Planning in Brooklyn, composed of Brooklyn businessmen. Purdy was personally interested in the larger problems of city planning and was a regular contributor to the annual conferences on city planning. McAneny, in addition to his experience with the City Club Committee on City Planning, was "very much interested in the broader subject of zoning as a part of the city plan." [23]

On February 27, 1913, McAneny went before the Board of Estimate with a resolution saying in part that

there is a growing sentiment in the community that the time has come when an effort should be made to regulate the height, size, and arrangement of buildings erected within the limits of the City . . . in order to arrest the seriously increasing evil of the shutting off of light and air . . . to prevent unwholesome and dangerous congestion . . . and to reduce the hazards of fire and peril to life.[24]

To meet these perils, the McAneny resolution provided that the mayor be authorized

to appoint a committee of three members of the Board of Estimate . . . to take this general subject under consideration, to inquire into and investigate conditions actually existing and to ascertain . . . whether, in their judgement, it is desirable to regulate the height, size, and arrangement of buildings hereafter to be erected . . . and to consider and report upon the question of the legal right of the City of New York to regulate building construction in the manner proposed. . . . Such Committee may also investigate . . . whether it would be lawful and desirable for the purposes of such regulation to divide the City into districts or into zones.[25]

The committee was to be called the "Committee on City Planning" and was to be empowered to appoint an "advisory" commission to be made up of "as many members as the Committee may determine, serving without pay" but, as a concession to borough autonomy, "including representatives of each of the several boroughs."[26]

In a separate paragraph of the proposed resolution, the Committee on City Planning was

instructed to submit, if practicable, in advance of any general report it may make, suggestions and recommendations with relation to the proposed limitation of the height of buildings on Fifth Avenue.[27]

McAneny's resolution was immediately and unanimously adopted by the Board of Estimate on February 27, 1913, the day it was introduced.

The resolution as passed was modestly worded. In effect, the board had committed itself to no more than determining whether zoning (or rather, the regulation of building heights) was a feasible and politic action.

In Mayor Gaynor's appointments to the Committee on City Planning, the pattern of borough autonomy was carried through —no city-wide officer was appointed. McAneny was made chairman of the committee and the presidents of Brooklyn and the Bronx, representing the other two most populous and intensively developed boroughs, were the other members.[28]

McAneny, as the initiating force in the proposal, took the lead and dominated the subject of zoning for the rest of his tenure on the Board of Estimate.[29]

By the end of the second week in April, the advisory Commission on the Height and Arrangement of Buildings (hereafter referred to as the "First Zoning Commission") had been appointed. McAneny and Bassett conferred closely on the composition of the commission; the other members of the Committee on City Planning apparently offered little but concurrence, so long as McAneny observed borough autonomy in making the appointments.[30]

McAneny had been instructed to select a commission that was representative of the boroughs; he also succeeded in achieving representation in occupational, interest group affiliation, and political terms. Nineteen men were appointed to the commission, with realtors, builders, manufacturers, labor leaders, and architects represented, as well as retail activities.[31] Republicans and "Independent Democrats" were in the substantial majority, although there were some Regular Democrats. As for borough representation: eight of the members were from Manhattan, five from Brooklyn, two from the Bronx, and one each from Queens and Staten Island. Purdy and Nelson Lewis, as officials of the city government, were nominally not representing any "local" interest.

The Fifth Avenue Association had two representatives on the Zoning Commission, and the New York Chamber of Commerce, the Bronx Board of Trade, the City Club, and the New York (Manhattan) Chapter of the American Institute of Architects were also among the interest groups represented.

It was, moreover, a commission whose members could claim to be "leaders." A list of their credits would include corporation presidencies, directorships, multiple memberships in high-prestige private clubs, and a diversity of activities that their primary professional occupations only suggested. Many were self-made, most were native-born New Yorkers, and most were still in their early middle years. As "successful" men they leaned toward conservatism, able to change their ideas but reluctant to do so when their own interests were touched.

During the week of April 13–20, the Zoning Commission held its first meeting in McAneny's offices. Bassett was chosen chairman, Purdy selected to be vice-chairman. Although it is probable that McAneny and Bassett had an idea of the direction they wanted the commission to take, the course of action was not so clear to the other members.

When the Commission first met, we had a lot of obvious problems and we had to do something about them. We hadn't been told what to do and we certainly didn't know how to do what needed to be done. And so we fumbled along with the idea of zoning in mind. It seemed to us that if we could allay the fear of damage to property, we could then get ahead.[32]

Purdy had already opened a campaign on tall buildings, using his expert knowledge to argue that skyscrapers injured realty values, were uneconomical to build, and that the days of laissez-faire building practices were no longer possible.[33] The press faithfully printed these attacks on tall buildings in their real estate columns.

But Bassett was haunted by another problem: the Board of Estimate had instructed the commission to consider if "districting" was legally possible, and Bassett the lawyer was unsure of the legal grounds on which zoning could be justified. On April 20, just after the first exploratory meetings of the commission, he expressed uncertainty over the means available to restrict building heights.[34]

The Fifth Avenue Association enthusiastically aided the commission in its investigations, gathering data on European and American precedents. The association had a strong interest in the outcome of the commission's deliberations, since the Zoning Commission had been specifically charged with the task of finding a solution to the Fifth Avenue problems. The Fifth Avenue Association and other groups met frequently with the commission and with individual commission members.[35]

Under Bassett's leadership, the Zoning Commission sent out feelers for support, for possible sources of opposition, and for inspiration. The commission mailed over 1,300 letters to various organizations and individuals and actively encouraged the submission—in person or in writing—of briefs, opinions, and comments.

The commission held conferences with members of the business community—financiers, insurance representatives, and the larger mercantile firms. Often these meetings were informal and intimate in nature. The purpose of the meetings were twofold: they allowed the commission to test the wind and they provided Bassett with the opportunity to use his considerable powers of persuasion.

The conferences bore fruit. By the end of June, 1913, the Federation of Churches, the Chamber of Commerce, and the Merchants Association came out in support of the commission's work.[36] At the same time, it was evident that the city was not to be taken by storm. On May 28, Ernest Flagg of the New York (Manhattan) Chapter of the American Institute of Architects (the AIA) admitted that control of some kind was probably needed, but he did not believe that the Zoning Commission was the way to approach a correct solution.[37] Flagg feared that the regulation of building heights would dangerously inhibit the city's growth.

Two weeks later, the New York (Manhattan) Real Estate Board offered a warning: the "chief trouble with the zone system" was the possible hardship it might work on investors in the future. The board hoped that the commission would "cautiously" approach regulation.[38] But the New York *Times,* perhaps overoptimistically, reported that the "consensus" was that some "system" of control of building heights was needed.[39]

The Fifth Avenue Association continued its appeals; members of the association regularly appeared before the commission and issued statements to the press. In July, fuel was added to the association's fire when the news was released that three "skyscrapers" of twenty stories each were planned between Thirtieth and Thirty-first streets on Fifth Avenue. The Association was "dismayed." [40]

The First Zoning Commission followed a slow and cautious policy, however. Time was needed—to convince the commission members themselves that regulation was necessary and desirable and to convince the interest groups represented on the commission as well as those that were formally outside its membership. And time was needed to discover legal and unimpeachable grounds for zoning.

The second week of July, 1913, Bassett announced that the weekly conferences that had been held with various associations and individuals would be discontinued for the summer. He said that many opinions had been offered, most of them favorable to regulation, but "much time is needed for the studies" of the commission.[41] Moreover, McAneny's valuable support was temporarily unavailable.

McAneny, the Manhattan borough president, was involved in the 1913 elections. The Regular Democrats were divided, and in 1912 had injured themselves by backing the wrong Democratic presidential candidate. The Fusionists were making a major effort to win control of the city's government, with John Purroy Mitchel as the mayoral candidate and McAneny as the candidate for president of the Board of Aldermen. The campaign was hard-fought, the stakes were high, and McAneny had very little time in which to worry about the Zoning Commission.

During the summer of 1913, while McAneny battled Tam-

many Hall, Bassett and Purdy undertook to bring the Zoning
Commission into line. The support of many of the groups represented on the commission indicated the success of Bassett's
efforts to date, but he wanted unanimity. Purdy told what
happened.

I drew up a resolution for the guidance of our committee which
we could quote to these fearful men [those worried that building
regulations would reduce land values]. This was not class legislation
of any sort. We were interested in helping both the rich and the
poor. When I tried to put through this resolution, one of the members of the Commission was suspicious of me, for don't forget, he
viewed me as a radical and was afraid that I was trying to put
something over on them . . . so action was deferred.[42]

Bassett and Purdy decided to rely on the police power as
the formal grounds for regulation and to use zoning as the
means to accomplish this regulation. A piece of dramatic stag-
ing was used to convince the commission:

Edward M. Bassett got the idea that it would be a good idea to
take our Commission to Boston and let them go over the records
right there on the scene [Boston had enacted its own heights of
building regulations relying on the police power]. . . . So we took
the entire Commission to the City of Boston and it made quite
an impression on them. We returned together on one of the Fall
River boats. We called them together and in a meeting aboard
the boat . . . got them, still very impressed by what they had heard
in Boston, to . . . adopt a resolution that they thought that zoning
was a lawful use of the police power. With this job accomplished,
the first part of our job was done—we had sought the answer to
our question of what to do and we had decided that the answer
was zoning.[43]

In the fall, the search for public approval was resumed. On
September 23, 1913, the New York (Manhattan) Board of
Trade submitted a brief to the Zoning Commission, agreeing
with the need for limitations and calling for early adoption.[44]
Early in October, the Brooklyn Chapter of the AIA came out

in favor of the principle of height limitations by "districting," and a month later a representative of the Manhattan Chapter of the AIA voiced approval of regulation.

By this time, Fusion had triumphed at the polls. In November, Mitchel was elected mayor, McAneny president of the Board of Aldermen, and the other members elected to the Board of Estimate were sympathetic to the Reform persuasion. And with the election over, McAneny could once again give his support to the work of the commission.

On December 5, 1913, the commission submitted the draft of its report to McAneny, who promptly said that he approved of the report in principle and in detail and that he would forward it immediately to the Board of Estimate for consideration.[45]

The report was an impressive document of 295 pages including appendixes. The first chapter was devoted to establishing the need for zoning, emphasizing the loss of light and air, the dangers to health, the loss of property values, the growing rates of fire insurance for high buildings, and the burden on the city's revenues and transportation facilities. The argument was neatly balanced with respect to aesthetics, economics, and "health and safety." This chapter was carefully aimed at two targets: to set the stage for invoking the police power; and to persuade the real estate, business, and financial interests of the city that the proposal would be a benefit to them.

The remainder of the report showed Bassett's fine legal hand. It was devoted to a discussion of the bases and precedents for relying on the police power. Other alternatives were considered —condemnation, limitations applied to segments of the city, nonregulation—and were rejected as either unrealistic or illegal. Bassett drew on foreign precedents (so carefully gathered by the Fifth Avenue Association) and on the precedents set in Boston and Los Angeles. His conclusion was inevitable: the city, if delegated the appropriate authority by the state, could regulate the heights and uses of buildings.

The report went on to say:

As the work progressed, it became evident that our report should emphasize, first, regulation of high buildings, second, districting, and third, Fifth Avenue conditions. No specific recommendations were made on factories and residences.[46]

The report admitted that there had been "diversity of opinions" but that "unanimity" had been achieved. "This report is not the result of compromises." [47]

At the same time, the report skirted some delicate issues. After a description of the horrible things that were happening in the Fifth Avenue area, the report said: "It was not considered practicable to make a preliminary report on Fifth Avenue conditions. The injury . . . is not an isolated problem." [48] Further, no direct suggestion was made as to the kind of regulation that should be used.

But the core of the report was in the appendixes. These included, first, a draft bill to go to the state legislature which would amend the Charter to enable the Board of Estimate to regulate the heights and uses of buildings. The second appendix was a draft resolution for the board which would continue the work of the Zoning Commission.

Apparently under McAneny's guidance, the draft bill was introduced in both houses of the legislature on February 27, 1914—just a year after the commission had been established. The bill floated through without difficulty:

It wasn't very difficult to get the Charter amended at Albany because it was recommended by the City officials. The legislature at Albany was very good and efficient about passing bills that were recommended by someone they respected, unless the bills happened to be of a political nature.[49]

On April 20, 1914, Governor Martin H. Glynn signed the

Charter amendment into law. The Board of Estimate was empowered to zone the City of New York.[50] With the governor's
signature on the bill, and with its report in the hands of the
Board of Estimate, the work of the First Zoning Commission
was completed.

The Second Zoning Commission: 1914–1916

The First Zoning Commission had won the necessary change
in the rules that would allow further action. But this was only
a first step. Although the Board of Estimate now had the legal
authority to zone the city, it had no explicit mandate to do so.
And although the First Commission had encountered little
opposition, there had been really very little to oppose: tech-
nically, and to a large extent actually, the commission had been
merely investigating ways and means. All men of "good will"
could endorse—in the abstract—limitations on the "evils" of
overbuilding, but actual limitations that might strike at pocket-
books and at customary ways of doing things were another
question.

The First Zoning Commission was a fairly complex and
effective communications network, reaching into the major
economic interests of the city, bringing these interests together
in a working body where they were subject to persuasion and
in their turn became persuaders. But there were limits on the
network. Large segments of the community had not been
reached: local civic groups, homeowners' associations, and
many business organizations had not been represented. Their
reactions, and probable actions, were still imponderables.

There were many propitious signs. The Board of Estimate,
after the November, 1913, elections, was a Reformer's "blue
ribbon" board. Mayor Mitchel was dedicated to the idea of
good government.[51] McAneny was still in a position of influence. The comptroller and four of the five borough presi-

dents were also Fusionists, "Independents"—Reformers. It was a board that could be expected to be sympathetic to proposals that promised a better city and a better government.

Real estate values were still scaling downwards. As Bassett was later to say, "The real estate owners were at a loss to know what to do with their property. They were looking at any angle as a talking point and they were more inclined to help along a promising plan like zoning." [52]

The Fifth Avenue Association, after an initial effort to capture the Manhattan borough president and the First Zoning Commission for its own purpose, had received no special treatment. That energetic and anxious body was tied to the future of zoning and it was clear that it could win its goals only by winning zoning for the entire city.

With the necessary enabling legislation passed, the first move was up to the Board of Estimate. The report of the First Zoning Commission provided the text of a resolution to establish a second commission "to recommend the boundaries of districts and appropriate regulations to be enforced therein." [53] Under McAneny's leadership, the proposed resolution came up before the board for consideration in May, 1914. [54]

The Board of Estimate scheduled public hearings on the proposed resolution for May 19, 1914. As the date neared, the Fifth Avenue Association stepped up its campaign in support of the resolution. On May 17 the association circulated a statement to the press and to as many governmental officials as possible. The statement asserted that Fifth Avenue, and New York City, had waited three long years and it was necessary to get on with the job. [55]

Bassett, as the now most publicized name in connection with "districting," spoke at length in favor of a second commission. [56] In spite of his persuasiveness, opposition arose. The United Real Estate Owners strenuously opposed the idea of limits. This group was apparently composed of small speculative and owner real estate firms, firms that had been the most seriously and directly hurt in the land value slump. They feared that an "arbitrary districting" would only worsen their situation, although the over-all tone of opposition was mitigated by the group's frank admission that some kind of limitation was needed. Ernest Flagg, claiming some support from members of the New York (Manhattan) Chapter of the AIA, registered his general objection. The Broadway Association, fearing the further depressing effect on land values that regulation might cause, also registered opposition.

Three days later, however, the board held a second and final hearing on the resolution, prior to voting. And the supporters were out in full force. In rapid succession, members of the City Club, the Fifth Avenue Association, the New York Chamber of Commerce, the New York (Manhattan) Chapter of the AIA (in spite of Mr. Flagg), and the New York (Manhattan) Real Estate Board rose to speak in favor of "districting," restricting the heights of buildings, and appointing a new commission to carry on the work.[57] The board voted immediately and unanimously to appoint a "Commission on Building Districts and Restrictions" (the Second Zoning Commission).[58]

On the same day, May 22, McAneny offered and had passed a resolution increasing the size of the board's Committee on City Planning to include all five borough presidents. This was insurance that borough autonomy would receive recognition in anything that the commission presented to the board.[59]

More than a month later, on June 26, 1914, the Second Commission was officially appointed. The representative character of the Second Commission changed very little from that of the First, although, of the sixteen members on the Second Commission, only seven had served on the First Zoning Commission.[60] The major occupational groupings—architecture, law, real estate, retail trade, manufacturing, and labor—were still heavily represented. Borough representation was carefully observed, in rough relation to population of the boroughs, and interest group representation changed little.[61] Party composition still consisted predominantly of Republicans and "Independent Democrats."

Bassett and Purdy once again occupied the two leadership positions, Bassett as chairman and Purdy as vice-chairman. The commission early organized into committees on a borough basis. These committees appear to have been symbolic, since the principal work of the commission was done in the committee of the whole or by Bassett and Purdy working with the six-man staff.

The Second Commission faced an immense and dual task. Its first labor was almost purely technical: gathering and digesting the data necesary to evolve a coherent districting plan. Some work had been done in this direction—the Fifth Avenue Association was brimming with information on its area; the Brooklyn City Planning Commission, under Bassett's leadership, had done some work; various city agencies, such as the Tenement House Commission, had information at hand—but no systematic effort to assemble or evaluate the data had been attempted before.

The second task was political: winning friends, convincing the dubious, generating interest, and quashing opposition.

The Second Commission attempted to solve both problems simultaneously. As Bassett recalled several years later:

One element of our success in New York was that the people handled all the zoning for the City. They told the Commission what to do. . . . The best zoning for any city is that zoning that the people of that locality [i.e., a specific area in the city] want to put on their property. . . . But one must add that there must be a period during which the owners can learn how these various things are apt to effect them.[62]

He went on to say:

That is one advantage in the zoners not knowing too much about it, because the people will be apt to supply that information that they don't know and it is a great way to get the people interested.[63]

The commission began a peripatetic career that carried its members, usually as a body, around the city. This practice publicized the work of the commission. The staff, meanwhile, worked in the streets, in the offices of the Tenement House Commission, the borough Buildings Departments, and other official agencies.

They [the commission] made a point of getting in touch with everyone who, through his experience or knowledge, they felt could assist. . . . They went out continually to meetings of local groups in the various parts of the five boroughs as well as inviting people who were conversant with local conditions constantly at the office.[64]

The staff went over every street and plot of land in the city. Bassett held literally a hundred meetings. They were advertised in store windows and on telegraph and telephone poles all over. Three hundred to a thousand people might attend some, only a handful others. He would answer their questions, meet hostility right there. . . . He was a beautiful speaker in front of people. He was always out to get this kind of grass roots support.[65]

The commission also moved to undercut potential opposition. It carried on a quiet and persistent campaign to win the favor of the financial institutions and to win the home-owners—the "people," the "grass roots"—by aiming at the homeowner's Achilles' heel: preservation of "neighborhood virtues." Over and over again, the commission emphasized that it "wanted to preserve the character of existing neighborhoods." [66]

The rest of 1914 was absorbed by these efforts—fact gathering and support gathering. In keeping with Bassett's strategy of exposure, the work was not rushed but was conducted at an almost leisurely pace.

During January, 1915, the Second Zoning Commission conducted hearings on its work thus far. The hearings were officially held by the Board of Estimate's Committee on City Planning and were sparsely attended, probably because the commission had very little yet to offer.[67] Burt Fenner, a member of the commission, took the opportunity to claim that he had found almost all architects generally favorable to the asserted goals of the commission. The New York Chamber of Commerce repeated its support. The Allied Realty Interests (a counterpart of the United Real Estate Owners but representing the large firms) said that a principal danger lay in setting limits on building heights that were too low.[68] Mayor Mitchel, when the hearings were over on January 28, instructed the commission to "take the comments of the speakers under advisement" in the preparation of the draft proposal.[69]

The hearings had been intimate, even casual, in atmosphere and apparently were primarily calculated to impress the mayor and the borough presidents with the support that the commission was beginning to generate.

Throughout the spring and summer of 1915, the Second Commission continued its research and quiet politicking, following the pattern set in the previous months. By the fall of 1915 enough had taken place to allow the commission to begin work on a preliminary report. On December 15 the commission announced that a tentative plan would be placed before the Board of Estimate early in January, so that public hearings could begin.[70]

This was to be the first test of the work of the commission. Prior to the publication of concrete proposals, discussion had dealt only in abstract principles. A written proposal would be a direct effort to convert principle into reality. It would be a potentially enforceable document that could directly affect the interests and aspirations of land- and homeowners, speculators, and businessmen for years to come. On December 16, 1915, McAneny was careful to announce that "many public hearings will be held upon the plan." [71]

"Shall We Save New York?"

Late in April, 1915, the Fifth Avenue Association had held a luncheon during which the main speaker pointed out that the loft invasion was continuing. He argued that the only satisfactory method of achieving protection would be the close cooperation of the owners and merchants on Fifth Avenue.[72] In January, 1916, after waiting for the report of the Second Commission, the association became increasingly impatient. In a lengthy statement the association complained bitterly. Fifth Avenue merchants had been patient, the association said; the Fifth Avenue Association had even been the prime mover in the process, but there had been no help forthcoming in nearly five years. There had been "many months of talk, investigation, compiling of statistics . . . what has become of the proposed ordinances?" Was it "lack of public support?" The "opposition of the real estate operators?"[73] Whatever the reasons, the association felt it had been waiting too long. The factory invasion was continuing and, even if a zoning code were passed, it would apply only to buildings "hereafter erected."

By January 25, 1916, the promised report of the Second Zoning Commission still had not made its appearance. On that date the Fifth Avenue Association held a luncheon to discuss strategy. J. Howes Burton, whose brother was a realtor and who was himself the principal owner of a major cotton goods firm, led the discussion. He said that he and other retail merchants were considering banding together to boycott garment manufacturers whose lofts were located above Thirty-fourth Street. "It is a radical step, and I believe it marks the first determined effort on the part of Fifth Avenue retail merchants towards fixing a clearly defined deadline."[74] He continued, "The Fifth Avenue Association feels that something must be done that has a punch in it."

McAneny was present at the meeting but refrained from any recorded comment on Burton's proposal. At a luncheon the following day, Walter Stabler (a member of the Fifth Avenue Association, the New York Real Estate Board, and the Second Zoning Commission) announced that he, at least, hoped Burton's plan would be a success. Stabler was also controller of the Metropolitan Life Insurance Company and, as a step toward implementing Burton's proposal, he said that Metropolitan would lend no money to manufacturers in the proscribed area.[75]

By the end of January, Burton, as the guiding light of the proposal, could say:

Practically all the retail merchants have agreed to join this movement, and it is no secret that many of the largest merchants, in joining the Fifth Avenue Association, have done so with the qualification that their membership ceases when manufacturing trades obtain a hold on this section [above Thirty-fourth Street].[76]

The Fifth Avenue Association was fighting not only for the economic survival of its members but for its survival as an organization. The association had deferred to the First and Second Zoning Commissions in the hope its interests would be served. Now the association was desperately trying to regain the initiative that it had lost.

Meanwhile, the work of the Zoning Commission continued. In a series of luncheons at the offices of the Merchants Association, first McAneny and then Walter Stabler spoke for the work of the commission. They were encouraged by the open and favorable commitment of two major mortgage and insurance companies.[77] The work of the commission to win the support of the financial institutions was bearing fruit. At the same time, however, a number of members of the Merchants Association complained that many potential supporters were receiving too little information to be able to take a public stand.[78]

On February 9, 1916, the Fifth Avenue Association announced that its Board of Directors had been expanded. Included in the new names were those of Burton and McAneny.[79]

A few days later, on February 20 and 27, the Zoning Commission released its tentative plans for Brooklyn, the Bronx, and Manhattan. These were only piecemeal sketches, presented in map form with little or no accompanying text, but it was obvious that the commission smarted from the accusation that it was failing to win supporters through a lack of publicity.

Almost at the same time, Bassett and Stabler made conciliatory gestures toward the Fifth Avenue Association. They agreed that the "preservation of Fifth Avenue was necessary to the trade interest of the city," they thanked the association for its efforts, and they said that a completed report would be ready in the second week of March.[80] Although the two organizations were working for the same goals, the association's fierce campaign threatened to eclipse the work of the commission.

By March 5, the Fifth Avenue Association had completed its plans. On that day a full-page ad appeared in all the metropolitan newspapers. The ad asked in bold print, "Shall we save New York?"[81] It asked if New York was to be saved from "unnatural and unnecessary crowding, depopulated sections, from being a city unbeautiful, from high rents, from illy . . . distributed taxation?"[82] The ad then went on to say that "the undersigned merchants will give preference to garment manufacturers located outside a zone" that had its southern limits at Thirty-third Street.[83] The notice was to go into effect on February 1, 1917. Thirteen of the most familiar and famous retail houses on Fifth Avenue signed the ad, and an additional list of endorsements included banks, mortgage houses, hotels, and clubs—all located on Fifth Avenue.

On the same day, Burton indicated that the Zoning Commission and the Fifth Avenue Association had reestablished their alliance and come to an agreement of mutual aid and benefit. In a press release, he said that real estate brokers had "fallen into line" and that he expected that the "Commission in the future will have no difficulty in carying out its plans."[84]

On March 8 the "Save New York Committee" (as it was now being called by the press) met and Burton urged the Zoning Commission to zone Fifth Avenue as soon as possible.[85]

In the meantime, the Advisory Council of Real Estate Interests (an organization of large real estate firms) called a conference of financial institutions to meet on the night of March 8. Bassett and members of the Zoning Commission staff were invited to explain their plans and solicit support. Seven financial institutions attended, and Bassett's powers of persuasion were successful.[86] An outgrowth of this meeting was a resolution, signed by fifty-three financial institutions, giving "hearty support" to the work and plans of the Zoning Commission.[87]

On March 10, 1916, the commission formally submitted its tentative report to the Board of Estimate. The board fixed dates for fourteen public hearings to be held during the months of March and April.

The preliminary plan was still very tentative. It divided the city into four types of districts: residential, business, unrestricted, and undetermined. The first two types of districts imposed definite height restrictions, the second two imposed no limitations. This draft was only a working document on which hearings could be based and more concrete negotiations could be conducted.

The response was marked. Under the impetus of the Broadway Association, Manhattan Borough President Marks appointed a "Broadway Commission," analogous to the earlier Fifth Avenue Commission.[88] Real estate owners on Fifth Avenue organized the "Central Fifth Avenue Committee" to support the zoning plan and to try to extend the Save New York Committee's boundary down to Twenty-second Street.[89]

As the hearings began, the complicated process of negotiation in public and private, of compromise, persuasion, and the soothing of doubts, got seriously under way.[90] The hearings increasingly revealed that any major doubts about the general principle of zoning had been quashed. The process became one of satisfying the concrete aims of specific localities and interests. Group after group appeared, certified their general support of zoning, and then got down to the real problem. For example, representatives from Greenwich Village split on the kind of restrictions they wanted: one group, led by real estate owners, wanted the Village left unrestricted. Another group, the Greenwich Village Improvement Society (made up of homeowners), wanted business activities to be sharply restricted. And so it went.

Bassett usually spoke for the commission, and his answers were normally noncommittal: he "made note of the request," promised consideration, and passed on to the next speaker. Frequently the commission asked for a speaker to file a brief or to confer with the commission in private.

The March hearings (held on March 27, 28, 29, and 30) were devoted entirely to Manhattan. The emerging pattern was clear. The local civic associations and homeowners' groups were eager to endorse the plan, but they were also eager to ask for larger and larger restrictive areas—to protect their neighborhoods, playgrounds, and parks. The business and real estate groups, whose support had obviously been won, struggled for room. Their chief concern was the boundaries of the unrestricted districts—do not limit the area available for growth, they argued. At points, the two differing sets of interests came into conflict, and the commission hoped to win the support of both.

It was evident, however, that the major part of the battle had been won. The procession of supporters was impressive and opposition came from dissatisfied individuals rather than from groups with large memberships. By the end of the Manhattan hearings the roster of supporters included the United Real Estate Owners, who had previously been in opposition (had the endorsement of the financial institutions made the difference?), and a number of groups which had hitherto been silent.[91]

The New York *Times* summed up the reactions in its real estate section when it said that "the plan was met with approval by almost everyone" and that the approval was based on "personal interest." [92]

On April 2, 1916, the mayor sent a letter to Burton's "Save New York Committee" indicating the first public announcement of support by Mitchel. The mayor said that he was in "thorough accord" with the goals of the committee and went on to say:

> The Save New York Committee is most opportune. It serves to emphasize and supplement the comprehensive plan for controlling city growth . . . that has been prepared in tentative form by the Districting Commission of the Board of Estimate.
>
> The supporters of the Save New York Committee deserve credit for calling attention so impressively to a prime need of the city.[93]

The first two weeks of April were given over to hearings for the outlying boroughs. In general the reactions were similar to those in Manhattan, with the exception of Staten Island. The Island had been zoned as largely unrestricted or undetermined (in recognition of its low level of urbanization), and the few homeowners who made the long trek from Staten Island to City Hall were there to complain that their borough was not being properly protected.

Although the reactions of groups from the Bronx, Queens, and Brooklyn were generally favorable, the homeowners' groups were especially wary about offering their support. These boroughs had broad areas classified as "unrestricted" or "undetermined," and the homeowners feared the invasions of business and manufacturing as well as "undesirable" residential elements. They gave their support, but it was a conditional support. They often asked for "reconsideration"—the Brooklyn Heights Association, for example, wanted the entire Brooklyn

Heights area restricted to residential uses; from the Bronx, Riverdale and City Island groups also wanted greater restrictions than offered by the proposal. At the same time, the local business groups, such as the Queens Chamber of Commerce, were "pleased" with the allocation of restrictions in their areas.

The public hearings closed on April 18, 1916. At this point, the Zoning Commission faced a mixed universe: few groups had met the proposal with totally adverse reactions, most had been in favor; but from those favoring, support was often tentative or conditional.

The commission had publicized the plan and had won a general endorsement, but much of the endorsement was based on the expectation of special concessions, especially to home-owners' associations. The Zoning Commission had done all that was formally required of it; it could now go to the Board of Estimate. But this would be a gamble. Too many groups might be too displeased for the members of the Board of Estimate to feel there was a mandate to impose a drastic innovation in public policy, and failure before the Board of Estimate would mean years of work wasted.

The commission chose another alternative: informal public hearings were scheduled for the latter part of April and for the whole of May (in all, twelve further hearings). These hearings were less "hearings" in the proper sense of the word than an opportunity for the commission to air "second thoughts" about its tentative plan. Group representatives once again trooped into City Hall with their specific complaints and requests.

Late in May, the Zoning Commission announced important changes, mainly items already mentioned in the informal hearings: factories would be restricted to the Twenty-third to Thirty-fourth Street area and as compensation substantial manufacturing areas were added in other parts of the city. These changes were admittedly the outcome of "conferences" with the Save New York Committee, the Central Fifth Avenue Committee, and "other interested business groups." [94] The commission was also "sympathetically" considering the suggestions of the Riverdale, City Island, and Brooklyn Heights groups for more restrictive districts in those areas.[95]

On June 2, 1916, the commission forwarded its revised tentative report to the Board of Estimate for consideration by the board's Committee on City Planning.[96] This committee handed the report to the Subcommittee on the Relation of the Proposed Plan to Other Plans of City Development, chaired by Nelson Lewis in his capacity as chief engineer of the Board of Estimate. The other subcommittee members were the borough engineers and several lesser officials. A second subcommittee was also established, the Subcommittee to Consider the Districting Resolution, composed of the tenement house commissioner, the fire commissioner, the superintendent of buildings from each borough, and the corporation counsel. Its purpose was to be sure that the various agencies of the city government were not overlooked in the provisions of the proposal.

The proposed zoning resolution contained in the report was not an elaborate document by later standards, but neither was it simple. It contained three types of provisions: use restrictions, bulk restrictions, and administrative provisions.

The *use restrictions* covered four types of districts: residential, business, unrestricted, and undetermined. The report assumed that "the development of unrestricted districts" would be largely "industrial." [97] The "undetermined districts," as their name would suggest, were those areas left for future classification: "the aim has been [in the undetermined districts] to give the greatest possible freedom of action." [98]

The resolution also proposed *bulk restrictions,* aimed at limiting the height and size of buildings within each of the use districts. The most restrictive bulk provisions were imposed on the residential areas of Brooklyn and Queens, the most lenient were set for the commercial and manufacturing areas in all five boroughs.[99]

In the *administrative provisions* of the proposed resolution, the commission set means of enforcing the code. The Board of Standards and Appeals, newly created, would hear all appeals from the restrictions zoning imposed.[100] The Board of Estimate was charged with amending the code, if necessary. In the event proposed amendments to the code were unpopular, the proposal established the "20 percent rule"—that is, if 20 percent of the property owners affected by the proposed change objected, the Board of Estimate would have to pass the amendment by unanimous vote instead of by a simple majority.

The over-all effect of the proposal was close to a direct response to the groups which had appeared before the commission. The homeowners, especially in Queens and Brooklyn, were guaranteed that few multistory, noncommercial buildings would rise in their areas. The business and commercial interests, on the other hand, were given generous room for expansion, especially in Manhattan and the "downtown" areas of the other boroughs.[101]

The administrative provisions ensured the participation of officials of the city government and the "20 percent rule" meant that a borough president, backed by strong local interests, could block "encroachments" on questions of "local concern."

The Board of Estimate set June 19, 1916, for the board's first hearing on the commission's proposal. The campaign to win public support for the proposal intensified as the date approached. Bassett spoke to a number of local retail associations and frankly admitted to the Broadway Association that "largely because of the Association's representations and briefs" the commission had excluded industry from the jurisdiction of the association.[102] And he made similar statements to the Fifth Avenue Association and other local organizations.

A few days before the beginning of the hearings, the subcommittees filed their reports. Their recommendations were highly favorable. Changes were made in the proposed resolution to give greater control to the borough presidents in administering the resolution, but the attitude of the subcommittee was expressed as follows: "In some cases it has seemed to us that the restrictions could well have gone further, but in few, if any, cases does it appear to us that they have gone too far." [103]

The principal task of the subcommittees had been to ensure the support of the agencies of the city government, and they had labored hard to do so. The borough engineers and building superintendents were comfortably accommodated in the proposal: discretion was left to the borough building superintendents to handle such matters as checking building plans to be sure proposed structures conformed to the Zoning Resolution; and the Tenement House Commission maintained jurisdiction over the plan where it applied to tenements.[104]

The hearings held by the Board of Estimate in June were largely a repetition of the commission's hearings, except that the number of supporters for the proposal was even greater.[105] A number of homeowners' groups requested still further protection for their areas, but the business, retail, and civic associations all seemed pleased. At the conclusion of the hearings, the board announced that one further hearing would be held on July 25 and, at the same meeting, the board would vote on the proposal.

In the next two weeks, activity centered on the borough presidents. The Committee on City Planning of the Board of Estimate entertained the requests and complaints of various groups and prepared its own final draft of the resolution. In submitting its report on July 18, 1916, the committee echoed the sentiments of the subcommittees:

Your committee has carefully considered the final report of the Commission and every protest and criticism in regard thereto that has been presented to the Board. The moderation exercised by the Commission in its plans is evidenced by the fact that a large proportion of the criticisms made . . . were that more restrictive regulations should be applied.[106]

The committee then appended its recommendations. The major change offered was the elimination of the "undetermined" district. Apparently this amorphous designation made the homeowners' groups the most nervous, since it was applied largely to areas that adjoined residential districts. Generally, the committee transferred the "undetermined" areas to residential use, usually in the most restrictive bulk categories.

The committee had also gone through a process of juggling use district boundary lines—most often in deference to homeowners and local business groups (Table 1).

TABLE 1. Use District Changes by the Committee on City Planning to the 1916 Zoning Proposal, by Borough

Change	Man-hattan	Bronx	Brooklyn	Queens	Rich-mond	Total
Residence to business	5	5	8	4	2	24
Business to residence	8	15	5	5	9	42
Business to unrestricted	3	2	1	5		11
Unrestricted to business	1	1	3	2	7	14
Residence to unrestricted					1	1
Unrestricted to residence					5	5

Source: Board of Estimate and Apportionment, Committee on City Planning, *Report*, July 18, 1916.

The committee conducted an equivalent process with the bulk restriction, although to a less extent. Manhattan had only one bulk change (to a more restrictive class), Brooklyn two, Queens two, and the other boroughs none.

When the hearings opened again on July 25, it was clear that almost complete satisfaction had been reached. Staten Island was the one exception. The meeting was sparsely attended; the Board of Estimate heard a few last-minute requests and made changes to accommodate them. When the vote was called, the Zoning Resolution was adopted, fifteen to one.[107] The one dissenting vote was from the borough president of Staten Island, who did not state his reasons. Apparently his negative vote was an expression of the feeling that Staten Island had been "underzoned;" there was too little protection to satisfy the homeowners' associations since close to three quarters of the Island was left unrestricted or in business categories. But the fact remained: New York City had a zoning resolution.

Summary

The Reform ideology, Fusion, the confused state of the real estate market, and the agitation of local interests were all ingredients that led to the final passage of the Zoning Resolution of 1916.

Fusion placed Reformers in positions of influence in the city government, and Reform provided the ideology that led to a "comprehensive" Zoning Resolution. Although the Fifth Avenue Association sought protection for its local interests, Bassett and McAneny—Reformer-like—turned this local problem into a means for seeking a "general and comprehensive" control of the city's building activities. Bassett and McAneny nonetheless made concessions to the political forces of the city. The borough presidents and the local and specialized interest groups all left their imprint on the final form of the Zoning Resolution of 1916. It is unlikely that the Reformers could have achieved zoning without considering borough and local interests, and Bassett and McAneny carefully used tactics that won the support of these interests.

II

THE YEARS
OF FRUSTRATION
1917–1945

The three decades following the passage of the 1916 Resolution saw the dominance of local and special interests in zoning matters.[1] This dominance can be directly attributed to a political system that linked interest groups and party politics to zoning through the Board of Estimate and the Board of Standards and Appeals. While the Reformers and their allies won a major victory when the City Planning Commission was established in 1938, its initial effort at comprehensive zoning failed.

The Interim Years: 1917–1936

In the twenty-year period that followed the passage of the Zoning Resolution, the politics of the city changed.[2] In 1917 the Regular Democrats reclaimed City Hall when Fusion was unable to meet the test at the polls. During the 1920s the borough party organizations flourished. The mayors of the 1920s (John F. Hylan, 1918–25; James J. Walker, 1926–32) often seemed to be little more than the pawns of the powerful Democratic borough "machines."

Borough party control gave the Reformers and the Fusionists little chance to be heard in the administration of the city. Their demands could be virtually ignored by the Regular Democrats who rode the full tide of the city's prosperity.

But the halcyon twenties ended in the Great Depression. For the Regular Democrats, 1931–32 brought scandal and the advent of a successful Fusion movement dominated by Fiorello La Guardia. La Guardia, a maverick Republican, was elected to the mayoralty in 1933. Through forceful leadership, attacks on the "machines," and shrewd management of the city's affairs, he retained possession of the mayor's chair until 1946. He achieved (or was able to claim credit for) a number of reforms, not the least being Charter reform in 1936–38. The Democratic borough organizations managed, however, to preserve a degree of their former health, often electing the borough presidents even when losing in the city-wide elections.

During the 1920s and early 1930s, the politics of zoning mirrored the localism of the politics of the city. The members of the Board of Estimate had almost complete hegemony in controlling the Zoning Resolution. Changes in the resolution stemmed from efforts by interest groups seeking a particular local advantage. The local chambers of commerce sought conditions favorable to local industry and trade, the retail organizations requested protection for or expansion of their areas, and homeowners fought the encroachments of commercial activities or apartment houses.[3] These requests were funneled through the borough party organization and the borough president's office to the Board of Estimate. "Borough courtesy" normally obtained on the Board of Estimate, that is, if the president of the borough concerned considered it politically advisable to vote for (or against) a proposal, the other members of the board would follow suit.[4] If an issue was cloudy—if the contesting nongovernmental protagonists had not arrived at a settlement, or if opposing sides were evenly balanced—there were means of delaying a vote until a solution appeared, usually by holding the question over for more hearings or "further investigation."[5]

A Brooklyn builder and engineer who was familiar with the

zoning system of the 1920s and 1930s responded to questions as follows in an interview with the author:

Question: How did the procedure work for the Board of Estimate during the 1920s?

Answer: The builder or the architect would have worked with the engineers in the borough president's office in the past. Let's say that you wanted a change in the zoning and came to me. I would talk to the borough engineer about the problem. I would show that rezoning was needed or you would lose the best use of your property. He would discuss it with his staff. He would then take it to the borough president for consideration on the Board of Estimate. It was usually very informal.

Question: What if there were objections from local property owners?

Answer: There might occasionally be. If that happened, then sometimes all the parties concerned could talk it over before the Board of Estimate met. Perhaps our lawyers would meet with theirs. . . .Sometimes these were big deals, with lots of people involved and civic associations, in which case the change often got delayed. But usually there were just a few people involved.

Question: Did you ever have help from local political leaders?

Answer: It depends on what you mean. The borough president is a political leader if you want to call him that. To be frank, there were those who could present a case more favorably, who understood the local situation and knew how to cut red tape, those who were concerned that local citizens got a fair hearing.[6]

There were other ways to find relief from the Zoning Resolution. The Board of Standards and Appeals (hereafter referred to as the BSA) was formally charged with granting "variances" to the zoning code (a "variance" was a relaxation of the provisions of the resolution in cases of "unnecessary hardship"). To a great extent, the BSA decided what constituted "unnecessary hardship" and, although an adverse decision could be carried to the courts on appeal, the BSA range of discretion was large.

The BSA became a source of political favors under the Democratic mayors of the 1920s.[7] Although the BSA served a rule-making, regulatory, and quasi-judicial function nominally, it was apparently easier to have this function performed in one's favor if the applicant for a change in the Zoning Resolution stopped by the local Democratic clubhouse first.

The builder and engineer continued:

> An owner might come to me and want to build a structure on his lot but the Zoning Resolution would not permit it. No other use than the one he wanted was feasible for the lot, however. I would go to the Board of Standards and Appeals and request a variance. I would show the owner was suffering a hardship, the lot was no good for anything but use to which he wanted to put it. . . .
>
> The procedure was usually we would toss the question back and forth. The board [the BSA] would study the code and maybe they would feel it was not feasible, not within the law. But we would talk about it informally.
>
> Question: How would it be settled?
> Answer: We would try to arrive at a reasonable settlement for everybody.
> Question: What about politics?
> Answer: Politics might be involved in a sense. If I knew someone, some of the right people, I would call them up, explain to them that the owner was suffering, that he was a good man and needed help.
> Question: What happened then?
> Answer: Then that someone would make some calls himself, or sometimes he might come by and speak before the board [the BSA] and usually there was some way of finding a reasonable settlement.
>
> You have to remember that these were local, small-scale problems, with local people involved. It takes many years, a lifetime, to understand the conditions in a particular locality.

As Tables 2 and 3 suggest, the pressures of the expanding city generated numerous demands for amendment to the Zoning Resolution. These were, however, largely local demands. The city's growth also led to calls for solutions to broader problems. In 1924, civic associations and business groups (led by the Merchants Association) asked for a permanent planning agency to devise means of combating traffic congestion.[8] With the election of the amiable "Jimmy" Walker as mayor in 1925, a City Committee on Planning and Housing was appointed. "The Committee of Five Hundred" was broadly representative.

It divided into subcommittees to handle the major problems of the city's development, including distribution of population, zoning, street planning, tenements, and industrial development.[9] Bassett and McAneny led the two subcommittees on zoning and on distribution of population respectively.[10]

TABLE 2. Amendments to the Zoning Resolution,
July, 1916, to December, 1940

Year	Number of amendments	Year	Number of amendments
1916	2	1929	55
1917	40	1930	45
1918	20	1931	23
1919	17	1932	22
1920	24	1933	12
1921	38	1934	25
1922	61	1935	15
1923	81	1936	12
1924	76	1937	26
1925	134	1938	50
1926	119	1939	41
1927	144	1940	48
1928	69		

Total: 1,371

Source: New York City Planning Commission, Annual Report for the Year 1940.

TABLE 3. Amendments to the Zoning Resolution, July, 1916, to December, 1940, by Borough and by Type of Amendment

Borough	TYPE OF AMENDMENT Use	Bulk	Total
Manhattan	102	21	123
Brooklyn	255	110	365
Bronx	117	19	136
Queens	392	121	513
Staten Island	56	6	62
New York City	922	277	1,199
		Miscellaneous:	172
		Grand Total:	1,371

Source: New York City Planning Commission, Annual Report for the Year 1940.

Both the City Club and the Citizens Union felt that a reasonable goal of the Committee of Five Hundred would be to outline plans for rezoning the city.[11] These organizations argued that the 1916 Resolution was too permissive and that too many provisions were now obsolete as a result of shifts in the land market. Further, conventional planning dogma held that frequent general revisions of zoning codes were necessary for good planning.[12]

The final output of the committee was bland.[13] Although there was very little in its report to please the Reform-oriented, Bassett and McAneny did recommend the establishment of a permanent city planning body within the city government.[14]

The City Club and the New York *Times* immediately backed the proposal.[15] The Citizens Union labeled the committee a "failure" and said that it "merely restated the old problems," but went on to endorse the recommendation for a city planning agency.[16]

On November 13, 1928, Mayor Walker appointed Bassett to study the problem and draft a bill that would embody a planning body.[17] Bassett offered his proposal early in 1929.[18] He proposed that the Board of Estimate continue to have final authority over city planning matters, but that there be a three-member City Planning Commission which would have initial jurisdiction over questions involving the city's physical development.[19]

On February 26, 1929, the Bassett proposal was introduced as a bill in the state legislature.[20] The borough presidents promptly construed the bill as a threat to their power. On March 11 the borough presidents had a "sharp clash" with Mayor Walker in the Board of Estimate over the Planning Commission Bill.[21] William Flynn, acting for the Bronx borough president, called it a plan for a "super-government." [22]

The battle was carried to Albany where, during March, hearings were held on the Bassett proposal. Walker and Bassett spoke in favor of the bill. George U. Harvey, Republican borough president of Queens, appealed to the Republican Senate majority leader. He argued that the bill would "build up a super-Walker government" and claimed that he spoke for the other borough presidents who were silent because they and Walker were all Democrats.[23]

The Senate Cities Committee favorably reported the bill out on March 26.[24] The fight on the floor then began to run against the proposal. The sponsor of the bill, a Democrat from Brooklyn, was not present to ask that the bill be called up for a vote. The Citizens Union representative tried to reach Walker to persuade him to take steps to have the bill moved, but without success.[25] The opportunity was lost, and the New York *Times,* reviewing the effort, attributed the failure to the opposition of the Brooklyn Democratic organization and a lack of drive on the mayor's part.[26] Borough autonomy had triumphed.

The issue did not remain dormant, however. The city-wide civic associations, led by the Merchants Association, continued to press for a planning body. On May 23, 1930, Walker introduced in the Board of Estimate a bill for a one-man planning department which would have no power over zoning matters.[27] It was obviously a compromise measure, and the Citizens Union said that the proposal "fell far short of an ideal set-up" and stressed the complete lack of powers of the proposed department.[28]

Early in June, 1930, the mayor's bill came up for consideration in executive session of the Board of Estimate. The word filtered out that the borough presidents had rejected the proposal, even in its watered down state. The mayor was reported to be "irritated" by this opposition.[29]

On June 26, 1930, the board voted on the bill. It was passed ten to six, with four of the borough presidents voting against it. Only Staten Island cast a favorable vote.[30]

The new City Planning Board proved to be totally ineffective.[31] In 1933, when the Board of Estimate approved the mayor's recommendation that the Planning Board be abolished as an economy measure, there was no one to mourn its passing.[32] As an object lesson, however, events had shown that the borough presidents would defend their prerogatives in zoning and that, without a strong impetus from the mayor and supporting nongovernmental groups, efforts to approach the city's physical problems from a "comprehensive" view would be opposed as threats to borough autonomy.

The City Planning Commission: 1934–1936

The idea of a city planning commission did not die easily. During the 1930s planning was in the air. The Great Depression stimulated talk of "planning": economic, social, and urban. In Brooklyn, Cleveland Rodgers, editor of the Brooklyn *Eagle,* organized a "ten-year plan" for Long Island.[33] When La Guardia became mayor in January, 1934, he had already promised to reestablish the Planning Board.[34]

The opportunity for the Reformers and their Fusionist allies to put La Guardia's promise into effect came with the establishment of a commission to revise the City Charter, a pet reform project. By 1935 there had already been an abortive effort to amend the Charter along Reform lines. And on January 12, 1935, La Guardia appointed a new Charter Revision Commission—one with power to have its proposals carried to the polls. The following month, he renewed his pledge to see a city planning commission established.[35]

The new Charter Revision Commission was strongly Reform in orientation. Its chairman, Judge Thomas Thacher, was a forceful politician and privy to the inner circles of the Reform movement. The other members were in varying degrees of sympathy with the Reform ideology.[36]

The crucial issue before the Charter Commission was centralization of the city's governmental functions. La Guardia was battling the borough Democratic organizations; the city-wide civic associations clamored for clear and centralized lines of authority molded after the Reform ideology. The borough presidents and their allies attempted to blunt an attack that might strip them of their authority in the politics of the city.[37] For the borough presidents, a central planning commission could only mean an attempt to reduce the administration of planning functions at the borough and local levels.

The Charter Commission began gathering data. It was slow to commit itself to the idea of a planning agency, although the Citizens Union early submitted a brief supporting a planning body, claiming that the Merchants Association, the City Club, and other civic associations endorsed the concept.[38]

Support also came from other sources. The Fusion borough president of Brooklyn, Raymond Ingersoll, said to the commission, "Some new setup would, no doubt, be desirable." [39]

The chief engineer of the Board of Estimate complained that the board was overworked with the details of zoning and went on to say: "The present tendency is to take away from the Board of Estimate some of the small matters such as zoning and vest them in a city planning body." [40]

By the middle of April, 1935, some of the members of the Charter Commission were showing a favorable disposition toward the concept of a city planning commission. On April 15, Borough President Harvey of Queens said to the commission:

There has been a great deal said about planning commissions and all that business. . . .If you have a City Planning Commission, keep it [made up of] the Borough Engineers. . . .Planning is a good thing.
Mr. Proskauer [of the Charter Commission]: That's why I want a City Planning Commission.
Mr. Harvey: But then, Judge, you will be stuck the moment you hit the Board of Estimate. You will never get plans through the Board of Estimate.[41]

And James Lyons, Bronx borough president, took a similar stand a few days later, saying impatiently that he was opposed to "super-bodies." [42]

By the time the commission heard from the president of Staten Island it was clear that the borough presidents (with the exception of Ingersoll of Brooklyn) had consulted and come to a common decision. On April 23, 1935, J. A. Palma, Fusion borough president of Staten Island, said he had held "conversations with the other Borough Presidents" on planning and related subjects and that he strongly favored borough autonomy.[43] The commission pursued the subject:

Question: The Borough Presidents on the Board of Estimate usually take the word of the Borough Presidents whose borough is affected, do they not?
Answer: They do, mostly.
Question: What is your atttitude toward a City Planning Committee or Commission?
Answer: I don't think you need one. I think that ought to be a borough function.[44]

On May 9, 1935, Mayor La Guardia testified to the commission. He was blunt: "This borough autonomy just cannot be ignored. . . . I would wipe it out entirely." He went on to say that there should be a city planning commission.[45]

La Guardia had made the lines of battle clear. The concept of a city planning commission could not be separated from the struggle between centralized authority and borough autonomy.

A week later, on May 16, 1935, the Charter Commission invited Bassett, as senior statesman of city planning, to address it. After sadly reviewing the failure of his earlier bill to pass the state legislature he said simply, "There is an insistence on borough autonomy in New York City." He argued further that the planning body must be closely linked to the mayor or "goodbye" to the planning commission.[46]

The Charter Commission was troubled by the opposition of the borough presidents. The day it heard Bassett, it held its first full meeting on the issue of a planning commission. One solution that it considered was a fifteen-man "advisory board" in each borough, to be appointed by the borough presidents.

It was suggested that this might "please" the borough presidents.[47]

By the first of June, 1935, the commission was still uncertain about the advisability of a planning agency. It was obvious that the idea generated opposition from the borough presidents, and the commission members may have wondered whether the concept was worth a threat to their hopes for a revised charter.[48]

On June 4, the other senior statesman of city planning, George McAneny, testified to the Charter Commission. He said there should be a "Bureau of City Planning" directly under the mayor; it should be a single-headed agency with purely advisory functions and no authority in zoning.

He was asked, "Don't you need continual planning? Nonpolitical planning?"[49]

McAneny answered, "If you set up an independent body, it might work more often badly than well."[50]

With this advice, the commission did not make up its mind easily.[51] By the middle of July, the commission was still uncertain. An unsigned memorandum of July 18, 1935, accepted the proposition that planning should be a city-wide function, but admitted that recognition had to be given not only to the "urge towards borough autonomy" but also to the "local urge within the boroughs."[52]

Throughout this period, the Charter Commission worked on the idea of a city planning commission with very little "assistance" from nongovernmental interest groups. Some, such as the Regional Plan Association, the Citizens Union, and the City Club, gave public support. Opposition came from the Queens Citizens Committee for Borough Autonomy (a body apparently inspired by the borough president's office in alliance with Queens businessmen) which objected to any and every proposal that threatened the borough president's prerogatives, but there was little additional comment.[53] The other groups that might well have been concerned (real estate organizations, building trades organizations, and business groups) were primarily involved in the complexities of proposals and counter-proposals to reorganize the fiscal structure of the city government and the administration of taxes and assessments. The abstract debate over a central planning body was weak stuff compared to the bread-and-butter aspects of other issues.[54]

In October, 1935, the scale within the commission tipped in favor of a city planning commission. One of the commission members, Joseph McGoldrick, suggested that the proposed capital budget should be administered by a city planning commission, and Chairman Thacher embraced this idea with enthusiasm. On October 1, 1935, the commission unanimously adopted this procedure.[55] The Charter Commission had committed itself to a city planning body.

The form of the city planning agency still had not been determined, nor where it would fit into the evolving governmental scheme. Three weeks later, on October 22, a solution appeared.[56] It was agreed that there should be a "City Planning Board." It would prepare a master plan for the city. There would be an advisory planning board in each borough appointed by the borough presidents. The City Planning Board itself would have seven members.[57] But the Charter Commission could not resolve the question of the composition of the Planning Board's membership; it failed to agree and passed on to more pressing matters.[58]

Two days later, on October 24, the City Planning Board was on the agenda again.

It was moved that zoning regulations should be set up by the City Planning Board, that it shall have power to make changes in zoning subject to certain terms and conditions. In the event of any change in zoning, this change must be filed with the Board of Estimate. If the Board of Estimate does not modify this by a two-thirds vote within a specified time, such changes will stand. This was passed.[59]

As the weeks slipped by, however, the Charter Commission—

perhaps troubled by the history of the Board of Estimate in zoning matters, perhaps prompted by the civic associations— moved to curtail further the powers of the Board of Estimate over zoning proposals. On April 8, 1936, the Charter Commission modified its proposed planning agency. In a report to its own members, the commission accepted the title of the proposed body as the "City Planning Commission."[60] This memorandum went on to argue that the Board of Estimate was too partisan and too borough-conscious to have a free hand over planning matters. The report said that the Planning Commission should have six members appointed by the mayor with the chief engineer of the Board of Estimate serving as a seventh and ex officio member. The first duty of the Planning Commission would be to prepare a master plan; the second duty, capital budgeting; and the third, zoning. Final decision on zoning questions would lie with the Board of Estimate, but it would require twelve out of the sixteen votes on the board to veto zoning proposals (that is, three fourths of the votes instead of the earlier two thirds).[61] The form of the City Planning Commission had finally been proposed.

On April 27, 1936, the Charter Commission released its preliminary report to the public. In it, the commission argued that city planning was a "special problem." To justify its proposal for a planning commission, the Charter Commission said:

Unfortunately . . . because of local and special pressures, and planning without relation to the city as a whole . . . great waste has resulted and a species of log-rolling has developed. . . . It is therefore proposed to create a responsible, independent commission concerned with the welfare of the whole city.[62]

The Charter Commission then began public hearings on its proposals, hearings that went on through May, 1936.[63]

Reactions to the Planning Commission proposal were mixed in the public hearings. The borough presidents (with the exception of Ingersoll in Brooklyn) repeated their opposition to the idea.[64] The League of Women Voters, the Merchants Association, and the Citizens Union, as well as the Regional Plan Association and the City Club, endorsed the proposal. The Bronx Board of Trade, the Bronx Chamber of Commerce, the Queens Chamber of Commerce, and the Queens Citizens Group voiced opposition. Staten Island groups were vociferous in opposing the proposed Charter as a whole and the Planning Commission in particular.[65] But few other groups showed any but incidental interest in the proposed Planning Commission and the vast majority of speakers passed over the topic without comment. Where group representatives did speak on the subject it was usually to deal with the Planning Commission as merely an aspect of the general problem of borough autonomy versus centralized governmental authority.[66]

Throughout the summer and early fall the intense campaigning for and against the proposed Charter went on.[67] Largely it was a struggle over the Charter as a whole, with the borough presidents fiercely attacking the proposal, while La Guardia, the Fusionists, the Reform organizations, and like-minded civic associations fought for its passage.

During the campaign, in spite of efforts to generate enthusiasm for (or opposition to) the proposed Planning Commission, this proposal faded into the background when compared with the issue of the powers of the mayor, the proposal to replace the Board of Aldermen with a City Council, and the reduction of the borough presidents' authority.[68] After an exciting contest, on November 3, 1936, the city voted to approve the proposed Charter, 930,000 to 600,000 (in round numbers).[69]

It would add drama to the story of city planning and zoning in New York City if it could be said that the creation of a City Planning Commission was the core issue of the Charter reform movement of 1934–36. Although many fought hard for a Planning Commission—the Regional Plan Association, the Citizens Union, and the City Club, to name only a few—the Planning Commission made its way into the city's governmental structure as a dimly seen "rider" on the Charter of 1936. Apparently few interest groups felt that they had a direct stake in the proposed functions of the Planning Commission or that the Planning Commission would threaten their stakes in performing its duties. There was, simply, little strong and no general response to the concept of a City Planning Commission.[70]

The Charter Commission had established a Planning Commission, but it could be argued that this new body was unquestionably a compromise solution. The new Planning Commission was an "independent" body. Although six sevenths of its members were to be appointed by the mayor, each member was appointed for an eight-year term and the terms of service were overlapping. It was therefore unlikely that any one mayor would appoint all the members. The Planning Commission would be protected from "political interference" by the Board of Estimate through the requirement that made a three-quarters veto of Planning Commission proposals necessary to stop action. The commission was, however, dependent on the Board of Estimate: for a vote on proposals and, further, for appropriations to conduct its activities. The borough presidents had opposed the Planning Commission concept, and in the future they might well act as a bloc against any agency that had come into being against their wills. And the "city-wide" officers on the board might feel they had very little stake in an agency over which they had no direct authority.

Neither support nor opposition to the Planning Commission had been general, hinting that the future success of the commission might depend less on the support of a clearly established constituency than on the policies it attempted to follow. Further, the Planning Commission was cushioned against "political" influences but was at the same time isolated from possible sources of political aid.[71] Given the opportunity

to cruise an independent course, the Planning Commission
might also be unable to find a sheltered harbor in case of storm.

First Efforts: The Tugwell Plan

On December 31, 1937, Mayor La Guardia announced his
appointments to the infant Planning Commission. Adolph A.
Berle, lawyer and "New Dealer," was named chairman with
the stipulation that he would serve for only an interim period.
Cleveland Rodgers, who had lobbied hard for the Planning
Commission in Brooklyn during the Charter campaign, was
one of the commissioners. Lawrence Orton, from the Regional
Plan Association, E. A. Salmon, an institutional architect, and
A. B. Sheridan, chief engineer for the Bronx, were other
members.[72]

The initial membership of the commission by no means
agreed on the function and role of the Planning Commission.
Was it to be an advisory body? And to whom? Was it to work
on a project-by-project basis with due deference to borough and
local concerns or was it to carry out what seemed to be the
Charter mandate of "comprehensive and general" planning?[73]

Berle, in his temporary status, was not anxious to commit the
Planning Commission to programs he would not be there to
follow through.[74] He turned to organizational matters, although agitation for action from the new agency began almost
as soon as it came into official existence in January, 1938.
Orton, prior to his appointment, had called for "sweeping
revisions" of the 1916 Zoning Resolution;[75] the Citizens
Budget Commission and the Citizens Union, in separate
analyses, listed zoning as a question of top priority before the
Planning Commission.[76]

On March 7, 1938, Berle resigned. The following month,
Rexford G. Tugwell, formerly professor of economics at
Columbia University and an important official in and close
adviser to Franklin Roosevelt's New Deal, became chairman

of the Planning Commission. Tugwell was a man of high intellectual attainments.[77] He was author of several books on economics and economic planning. Although waning in influence in Washington, he brought with him (for better or for worse) the mystique of the New Deal and Rooseveltian politics. He was "brilliant and stimulating" and unquestionably "courageous."[78] But his strength of character, and the fact that he expressed himself better through the written word than the spoken, were not always political assets. He occasionally was adamant where it might have been more politic to negotiate. Tugwell brought one further attribute to his office: a firm faith in planning—planning for the "general interest" as a legitimate, necessary activity of government in a complex industrial and urban society.[79]

In the late summer and early fall of 1938, the Planning Commission had its first skirmish with the borough presidents. The commission's request for staff was blocked in the Board of Estimate, and it was not until the Regional Plan Association, the Citizens Union, and other civic associations lobbied intensively for La Guardia's support that Tugwell's initial request was granted.[80]

Tugwell's interest in general, comprehensive planning led him to aim the efforts of the Planning Commission in two directions. The first program was the preparation of a master plan for the city; the second, the intermediate step of bringing aspects of the 1916 Zoning Resolution "up to date." Throughout the last half of 1938 and the first part of 1939, the commission and its staff devoted most of its attention to zoning revisions.

On May 3, 1939, the Planning Commission officially released the new zoning proposals. These proposals were far from comprehensive. The plan was to establish two new use districts[81] and to correct what Tugwell considered a major flaw in the 1916 Resolution. To accomplish the latter, a special section of the proposals excluded flashing signs and billboards over a certain size from retail districts. This section continued, however, by saying that existing signs and billboards that did not conform to the new provision would have to be "amortized"—that is, removed after a limited period of time.

On May 24 the Planning Commission began public hearings on the proposals. Turnout was light and reactions were mild. The majority of groups addressed themselves favorably to the new use districts. Two local business groups (the Central Mercantile Association and the Thirty-fourth Street Midtown Association) were troubled about what the sign prohibition might do to local retail activities. Forty-nine telegrams were received from "employees of outdoors advertising companies" protesting the sign provisions.[82]

More hearings were held on June 1 and June 5, and the turnout was larger. Reactions were still mixed. The Merchants Association, the Regional Plan Association, and other lesser names favored the proposals on the basis of the new use districts. The Brooklyn and Bronx Real Estate Boards called for delay until there was time to study the proposals. The Fifth Avenue Association admitted that it was uncertain what stand to take on the question.[83]

On June 14, 1939, the Planning Commission adopted a revised version of the plan. The main provisions were the same, except the "nonconforming use" provisions for signs and billboards were spelled out more clearly.[84] This appears to have been in response to Tugwell's growing conviction that the Resolution of 1916 had no provisions for "extinguishing" nonconforming uses and that an effort in this direction "weighed upon the Commission as a duty." [85]

The effect of the revision was to make the issue clearer. By the end of June a number of groups, especially the Queens and Brooklyn Chambers of Commerce and the Bronx Real Estate Board, came out in opposition to the "retroactive" nature of the principle involved.[86] On June 30, Frank Barrera, a young lawyer speaking for the Brooklyn Real Estate Board, joined this opposition.[87]

With the end of June, the Planning Commission suspended further hearings until the fall. The pattern was confused. It was obvious that many groups were uncertain what the Planning Commission was proposing: was this simply an attack on signs and billboards (which many admitted were "eyesores")? Or was it the introduction of a new principle—one which, if accepted, could eventually be applied not only to signs but to any kind of nonconforming use? The New York (Manhattan) Chapter of the AIA still accepted the former viewpoint, as did a number of local retail associations. The City Club favored the proposals strongly. On June 30 the Fifth Avenue Association moved from the column of waverers to the side of those favoring the proposals.[88]

Early in November, 1939, the Planning Commission scheduled new hearings for November 22. On November 15 the Twenty-third Street Association held a special meeting to consider the proposals. The association voted, nearly unanimously, to oppose the commission's plan; according to the chairman of the association's zoning committee, the plan was "dangerous."[89] By November 19, other groups prepared similar releases for the press. The New York Real Estate Board admitted it was still working on the subject, but the Brooklyn and Bronx Real Estate Boards repeated their opposition. Frank Barrera, spokesman for the Brooklyn board, argued that the nonconforming use provisions would hurt small enterprises and seriously damage land values.[90]

The second round of hearings began on November 22 with the opposition present in full force. The Staten Island Real Estate Board joined its sister boards, although the New York Real Estate Board only objected to matters of wording and said it accepted the general content of the proposals. The

Citizens Union made an appeal on behalf of the revisions and commended the Planning Commission on its efforts. There was, however, little other suppport.[91]

In the following days, more hearings were held, and the New York Real Estate Board began to show doubts. Its spokesman said that a fundamental blow "against land values was at foot in the new retroactive provisions."[92] The Bronx Board of Trade sent a letter to La Guardia saying that some "good work" had been done but that the nonconforming use provisions represented "confiscatory" powers.[93]

As 1940 grew closer, the opposition solidified. The Planning Commission was now conducting studies for the formulation of a master plan. This meant there was little staff time available for "field work" on the zoning issue. Apparently small effort was made to contact interest groups, to persuade them, or actively to seek sources of potential support. The Planning Commission was playing a lone hand, whether by force of circumstances or by choice is less than clear today, but the effect was the same—even the few groups that might have been supporters were in danger of being lost.[94]

By the end of January, 1940, the Planning Commission concluded its hearings. They ended on a somber note: the New York Chamber of Commerce and the Regional Plan Association both expressed sympathy with the principles of zoning but said that the "retroactive" provisions had to be opposed.[95]

Early in March, 1940, the Planning Commission released its annual report. Tugwell said in the report that the 1916 Resolution "should be completely rewritten."[96] He then went on to say that the activities of the real estate community were the major causes of "deterioration and the spread of slums."[97] A few days later, the New York *Times* editorially pondered the problems confronting Tugwell and the Planning Commission. It pointed out that Tugwell had said that the Planning Commission was in "the heart of a cyclone of private interests."

The editor asked: Does the Chairman find the public interest and private interests irreconcilable? And he then answered his own question: yes.[98]

On May 29, 1940, the Planning Commission met to vote formally on the proposed amendments to the Zoning Resolution. It was a heated meeting. Two of the commissioners, Sheridan and the ex officio chief engineer of the Board of Estimate, submitted a minority report which advocated deleting the nonconforming use provisions from the proposal. The commission, however, adopted the plan without revision by a four to two vote.[99] The proposal was then forwarded to the Board of Estimate, which set June 20 as the date for its hearings on the plan.

In the intervening three weeks, a steady stream of objections poured into the Board of Estimate and were released to the press. Almost without exception the objections were to the "confiscatory" nonconforming use provisions.[100] Frank Barrera, acting for the Brooklyn Real Estate Board, offered a line of compromise, however. He suggested that if the Board of Estimate would accept Sheridan's minority report—thereby deleting the nonconforming use provisions—the Brooklyn Real Estate Board, for one, would enthusiastically support the rest of the proposal.[101]

The Broadway Association recommended the same procedure in a letter to the Board of Estimate. The association suggested that the board return the proposal to the Planning Commission with instructions for the commission to hold a joint study with "concerned interests." It argued that such a joint study might lead to a satisfactory solution for all the participants.[102]

The Board of Estimate held its hearings on June 20, 1940. It was a stormy session. The meeting was picketed by representatives of the sign painters' and electrical workers' unions. Borough President Cashmore of Brooklyn read a prepared statement opposing the plan. The Planning Commission refused the offers made by Barrera and the Broadway Association. La Guardia was absent from the meeting and, after a series of delicate maneuvers, the Board of Estimate voted to reconsider the plan at a later meeting. All the borough presidents except Stanley Isaacs (Republican) of Manhattan voted to defeat the plan in its entirety, but the final vote was eleven to five to reconsider.[103]

The New York *Times* concluded that the board had acted "wisely" in delaying a final decision. The opposition might have "merit" on its side and did not represent an "attack on zoning or the City Planning Commission" per se.[104] It was clear, however, that most groups were unwilling to accept as radical an innovation as nonconforming use provisions. The opposition boardered on unanimity and cut across diverse interests. There was little or no response from the homeowners and the Planning Commission had done little to encourage support from the city-wide civic associations—the opposition of the Regional Plan Association and the silence of the Citizens Union and City Club were evidence of this failure.

On June 25, 1940, the Board of Estimate met in executive session to consider the proposals. Information leaked that the city-wide officers accepted defeat on the nonconforming use provisions to win passage of the new use districts.[105] On June 28 this was borne out in fact when the board voted unanimously to pass all the provisions except those related to the nonconforming uses—and these were defeated without a dissenting vote.[106]

The Planning Commission could claim a partial victory. The new use districts represented an "updating" of the 1916 Resolution, but Chairman Tugwell's primary aim had been defeated. It seemed clear that the interest groups and the borough presidents would accept a "moderate" revision of the zoning code, but "radical" revisions would be met with powerful opposition.[107]

Chairman Tugwell was to resign a year later, on July 26, 1941. In the intervening months he offered his master plan, the product of close to three years' work. Robert Moses attacked the plan and others greeted it either with indifference or with open hostility. The master plan was finally shelved by the Planning Commission in February, 1942, and zoning continued to serve as the functional equivalent of comprehensive planning in New York City.[108]

The Moses Plan: 1944–1945

Tugwell resigned from the Planning Commission in July, 1942, to become chancellor of the University of Puerto Rico.[109] La Guardia allowed the vacancy on the Planning Commission to stand until after the November elections. On November 23, 1942, the mayor announced that E. A. Salmon, already a member of the commission, was to be chairman, and Robert Moses would fill the seat vacated by Salmon.[110]

Moses came to the Planning Commission with no real sympathy for the goals Tugwell had attempted to set.[111] Moses saw city planning as a matter of meeting the city's needs on a project-by-project basis,[112] and he never gave his full attention to the activities of the Planning Commission, using it chiefly as an additional source of information and as a public forum for his own individual brand of planning. The new commissioner did bring with him a reputation for being a fighter, and he also brought La Guardia's good opinion. And, in 1944, Moses emerged as the focal figure in a bitterly fought contest over extensive rezoning of the city.

On May 28, 1944, the Planning Commission released a proposal for a modification of the bulk restrictions for the entire city. The commission saw the occasion as auspicious:

World War II prevented much private or public construction, and "a revival of building is expected as soon as materials and labor are again available. In the coming period of activity we must guard against a repetition of past mistakes."[113] The proposal, as formulated by Moses, was sharply to increase bulk restrictions for all use districts for the entire city.[114]

The first hearing for the new plan was set for June 28, 1944. During the Planning Commission meeting on June 14, Commissioner I. V. Huie objected to the proposal, however. Commissioner Huie argued that insufficient "field work" had been done on the proposal and recommended that the amendment wait until there had been "consultation" with interest groups and an estimate made of the probable consequences of the proposal.[115] The commission overruled Huie, however, and the hearings were held on June 28 as scheduled.

The first reactions were tepid. The Citizens Budget Commission and the Commerce and Industry Association (the Merchants Association under a new name) asked for more time to study the proposal. Bassett was present with praise for the plan. The Citizens Union and the City Club both endorsed the proposal. A number of mortgage houses, however, were worried that the cutback in bulk might lead to a loss of investments, but they were almost alone in openly expressing concern.[116]

The Planning Commission held a second hearing on July 12, 1944. Moses led the proceedings. He interrogated opposing speakers and pressed for an early decision on the plan. Although the objections were initially mild, debate became more heated as the meeting progressed. The New York Real Estate Board protested that the cutbacks in bulk might reduce both land values and rental values and, as a consequence, hurt real estate owners and developers. The majority of groups asked for more time for study. The Planning Commission, however, set August 1—only half a month away—as the deadline for filing protests. The New York (Manhattan) Chapter of the AIA objected strenuously to this "arbitrary" limit. The New York Real Estate Board complained as bitterly.[117]

Pressure for further hearings built up during August. The New York Chapter of the AIA, the New York Chamber of Commerce, the Fifth Avenue Association, and the Commerce and Industry Association filed objections to the plan and requests for further consideration, hinting that their opposition before the Board of Estimate would be the price of failure to accede to their requests.[118]

On August 30 the Planning Commission bowed to the pressure. It agreed to reopen the hearings on September 13. At the same time, the commission made revisions of the proposed bulk restrictions for Manhattan,[119] perhaps hoping to forestall the attacks of Manhattan-based groups.

The September 13, 1944, hearings were once again heated. Commissioner Huie offered a counterproposal to the commission's plan. He suggested that bulk restrictions be relaxed in those areas where land values were high (primarily Manhattan and commercial and industrial areas in other boroughs) and that bulk restrictions he made "realistically" severe in one and two-family residential areas.[120] Huie's compromise proposal had a dual appeal: it was an attractive offer to groups whose members had heavy investments in high-value commercial and industrial property, while homeowners might find increased bulk restrictions in their areas appealing. The Planning Commission, however, voted against holding hearings on Huie's proposal.[121]

There was evidence that the arena was broadening, however. Some groups were turning to the borough presidents for help. Spokesmen for the borough presidents of Manhattan and Queens asked the Planning Commission for time to study the proposals.[122] The commission did not take action on the Moses plan at the September 13 meeting, but neither did it agree to continue the hearings.

On September 28 a meeting was held in the offices of Manhattan Borough President Nathan. Members of the New York Real Estate Board, the Bronx Real Estate Board, and some local retail associations were present. They discussed ways to generate support for Huie's proposal, and the Bronx Real Estate Board representative argued that a general committee should be formed since "many interests are working at cross purposes." [123]

By September 30 the idea was put into effect. On that date the Citizens Zoning Committee came into being.[124] The organizational work had been underway for some time; the task had not been a simple one,[125] but the new committee could initially claim eighteen members representing the five boroughs and many interests.[126] The first statement of the Citizens Zoning Committee (hereafter referred to as the CZC) was mild, saying that the amendments before the Planning Commission were

so sweeping in their nature they constitute in effect a new zoning law—the first since the adoption of the present Zoning Resolution in 1916. [The amendments] may be ill-advised and need more study.[127]

In a meeting of the CZC on October 2, 1944, Robert Dowling was chosen to act as executive secretary.[128] Dowling, speaking for the CZC, aimed his appeal at the building and business interests that had already shown alarm at the Moses plan. He said that the committee opposed the Moses plan because the proposal would handicap construction, reduce land values, and increase business costs.[129]

The Planning Commision met on October 4. Borough President Nathan, in a letter read to the meeting, called for a hearing on the Huie proposal. The Planning Commission was

meeting to discuss matters unrelated to the Moses plan, and
Chairman Salmon ruled that the CZC could not speak on
Commissioner Huie's proposal. The Citizens Zoning Committee announced it would carry its objections to the Board
of Estimate.[130]

By this time, the CZC had successfully coalesced its diverse
aggregation of interests around the issue of bulk restrictions
on business districts. But the Planning Commission was also
engaged in mustering support, primarily through the Citizens
Union, the City Club, and the Womens City Club.

On November 1, 1944, the Planning Commission met to
vote formally on the Moses plan. Commissioner Huie alone
voted against the proposal, and the Planning Commission
forwarded the plan to the Board of Estimate.[131]

The Board of Estimate began its hearings on November 15.
Prior to the hearings, the Citizens Union and the Womens City
Club held a rally to indicate support for the Moses plan. Moses
spoke to the rally, castigating the opposition. Those who
attended were pleased by the support that the rally demonstrated.[132]

The board's hearings lasted for six hours on November 15.
There were thirty speakers, and the majority were in opposition. Moses acted as the principal defender of the plan. But
the opposition had increased in numbers, and the Board of
Estimate postponed voting on the proposal.[133]

During the two weeks before the Board of Estimate cast
its final vote, there was a flurry of activity and negotiation.
The CZC, working with Huie, tried to arrange a compromise.
The CZC notified the Board of Estimate that Huie was willing
to modify his proposal toward more restrictive bulk controls
if the board would give the proposal consideration.[134] At the
same time, La Guardia acted as a mediator for the Planning
Commission. On November 23 the mayor released a letter in
which he and the Planning Commission agreed that, if the

Board of Estimate passed the Moses plan, the Planning Commission would immediately offer an amendment that would relax the new bulk restrictions for a few retail areas.[135] The Citizens Zoning Committee, however, rejected the proposed compromise as inadequate.[136]

The CZC had one further strategy. A week before the Board of Estimate's final vote, the CZC revealed that it had been collecting signatures for a protest against the proposal—a protest based on the rarely used "20 percent rule" that required a unanimous vote of approval on the Board of Estimate if 20 percent of "affected property owners" objected to the proposed zoning change.[137] Dowling claimed that well over 20 percent had been achieved for the midtown area of Manhattan and that a similar effort was being made in downtown Bronx.[138]

In spite of the protest signatures, the Board of Estimate held its final vote on the Moses plan on November 30, 1944. The board split ten to six, with the borough presidents of the Bronx, Manhattan, Brooklyn, and Staten Island voting against the proposal and the city-wide officers and the Queens borough president voting in favor.[139]

The Planning Commission had apparently won a major victory. Although it was opposed by an organized and wide set of interests, with the aid of Moses and his excellent relations with the mayor the Planning Commission had seemingly triumphed over seven years of frustration.

Dowling and the Citizens Zoning Commission did not abandon the field, however. The day after the Board of Estimate's vote, Dowling announced that the CZC would go to the courts to test the "20 percent rule" as soon as it found a suitable case.[140] On December 29, 1944, the 431 Fifth Avenue Corporation filed to test the zoning amendment.

The result was almost anticlimactic. Although the Citizens Union filed an *amicus curiae* brief on the side of the Planning Commission, the State Court of Appeals held that the "20 percent rule" applied and that clearly the Board of Estimate had failed to pass the amendment by a unanimous vote.[141] The Planning Commission had won before the Board of Estimate on a split vote, but it was defeated by another "formal rule of the game," a rule that demonstrated the importance of the borough presidents' votes when coupled with an energetic opposition to zoning innovation. Moses characteristically commented on the outcome, "Apparently we were too far ahead of the procession."[142]

Summary

The twenty-eight-year period following the passage of the 1916 Zoning Resolution was dominated by one theme: the frustration of the "comprehensive and general" approach to zoning questions. Until 1938 there was no formal voice for comprehensive zoning in New York City. The zoning system functioned through the relations between interest group and borough president or interest group and the Board of Standards and Appeals.

In 1938, however, the Reformers won a major victory in establishing the City Planning Commission. This was to be the "nonpolitical" voice of the "general interest" and, by planning for the city as a whole, would overcome the 1917–38 patterns of localism, borough autonomy, and "borough courtesy."

The Planning Commission attempted to fulfill the role given to it by its founders. First in the Tugwell plan of 1938–40 and then in the Moses plan of 1944–45, the commission attempted zoning innovation and revision. Its "independence," its lack of a constituency, and the complex forces of interest groups and borough politics resulted in failure for these efforts.

III

REZONING
NEW YORK CITY
1945–1960

In the fifteen-year period following the end of World War II, the New York City Planning Commission made two attempts at comprehensive rezoning of the city. The first of these failed. The second effort, however, was attempted in a political atmosphere that seemed favorable to the Planning Commission's goals and was carried through to a "victory" for the commission in 1960.

The Post La Guardia Era

The second half of the 1940s, together with the 1950s, represented a period of change for New York City. Physically, the city underwent a building boom.[1] There was a steady expansion of the real estate market and an increase in population for some boroughs that was only partly offset by the move to the suburbs.[2]

In addition, the La Guardia era had had significant effects on the politics of the city. La Guardia expanded the civil service, thereby reducing the amount of patronage available to his successors. Although there were ways of evading civil service classification, the number of jobs open to reward the party faithful was reduced, and with this reduction there was a loss of incentive for partisan activity and of means to control the party organization. Further, the bureaucrat was increasingly replacing the party leader as a source of information and help when the citizen or the interest group was confronted with a problem.[3] Even so, the borough party organizations preserved much of their viability.[4]

The mayors of the post La Guardia era showed increasing independence. Although still forced to bargain with the other members of the Board of Estimate, the postwar mayors appear to have had a greater chance of success in asserting their claims than had either Hyland or Walker. And, of the three postwar mayors, William O'Dwyer (1946–50), Vincent Impellitteri (1950–53), and Robert Wagner (1954–), Impellitteri and Wagner had sources of electoral strength outside the Regular Democratic organization. Impellitteri ran against a Regular candidate on his own ticket in 1950 and won. Wagner defeated a Regular Democrat for the nomination in running for a third term in 1961 and went on to win the election.

The city was in a period of change. But the city agency primarily responsible for controlling physical change seemed completely unable to carry out its Charter mandate. The City Planning Commission had been defeated on both the Tugwell plan and the Moses plan, and the few groups that were its occasional supporters, such as the Citizens Union, the Regional Plan Association, and the City Club, were impatient with the commission's ineffectiveness and uncertain whether it deserved their support at all.[5]

The Harrison, Ballard, and Allen Plan

On October 24, 1947, Mayor William O'Dwyer announced that Robert F. Wagner, Jr., was appointed to fill the position of chairman of the City Planning Commission.[6] Wagner's appointment was not expected, but he seemed qualified to hold the position.[7] Son of an illustrious United States Senator, he was a skilled and rising "Regular" in the Democratic party.

Prior to his appointment to the Planning Commission, he had been a commissioner in the Department of Buildings.

On November 1, 1947, the new chairman took office. And, two months later, Mayor O'Dwyer announced that he and Wagner had concluded discussions on a major revision of the Zoning Resolution. The mayor had directed Wagner to begin work on a comprehensive rezoning of the city.[8]

A number of civic associations agreed that rezoning was desirable—the Regional Plan Association, for one, had been pressing for greater activism by the Planning Commission.[9] Further, Wagner was probably anxious for his tenure on the Planning Commission to be an aggressive one. He seemed to have O'Dwyer's support for preliminary studies, and the mayor himself was interested in having the Planning Commission do well.

On February 18, 1948, Wagner announced that machinery was being set up to undertake the studies necessary for comprehensive rezoning. And, on April 8, the Board of Estimate received a resolution from the Planning Commission requesting appropriations to hire the architectural firm of Harrison, Ballard, and Allen to conduct the zoning survey and prepare a plan for rezoning.[10] The board deferred action, however. Robert Moses threw his weight against the proposed appropriations, and the mayor was uncertain whether his official approval should continue.[11] Wagner lobbied for the zoning revision study both in public and with the mayor, and on May 13, 1948, the Board of Estimate voted to approve funds for the study.[12] The following day the New York *Times* editorially approved the board's vote and pointed out that it was time the Planning Commission did something to justify its existence.[13]

In the following months the Planning Commission made efforts to keep zoning in the public eye, but with small success. In November, 1948, Wagner asked for suggestions from interested groups,[14] but there was little response. Part of the difficulty appears to have been that the Planning Commission staff was not used to proselytize the public and the consultant firm was too busy with the required studies to fill the vacuum.

The Planning Commission began to falter in its resolve. Wagner became the Democratic candidate for the Manhattan borough presidency in the 1949 campaign and, although the consultants continued their work, neither Wagner nor O'Dwyer gave his attention to zoning.[15]

Wagner won the election for the borough presidency, and his duties as chairman of the Planning Commission came to an end in December, 1949. Late in December, Mayor O'Dwyer—who had successfully run for a second term—announced that Jerry Finkelstein would be the new chairman. Finkelstein was thirty-six years old and had been trained as a lawyer.[16] His career included work on Dewey's rackets investigations staff and on the New York *Mirror,* and he had founded his own trade paper for civil service employees. More important, he had acted as O'Dwyer's campaign manager, and his relations with the mayor were politically close and personally congenial.

Finkelstein opened his tenure with a request for large budget increases: a threefold increase of funds available for both staffing and planning programs.[17] He argued that the increase was necessary if the Planning Commission was to play a major and guiding role in the city's development.[18]

O'Dwyer scaled Finkelstein's request to more modest levels, but the mayor supported an increase. The Board of Estimate voted to give the Planning Commission chairman additional funds in accordance with the mayor's request.[19]

In May, 1950, Finkelstein turned his attention to the lagging zoning revisions. On May 8 he released a letter from O'Dwyer in which the mayor firmly supported the comprehensive zoning surveys.[20] This made it clear that Finkelstein had the support of the mayor, and, at the same time, Finkelstein announced that progress had been made by the consultants in preparing a final report.

On August 12, 1950, however, the New York *Times* expressed a growing discontent:

Statements from the City Planning Officials indicate the consultants have drafted their rezoning plan and that the proposal is known in detail to many. . . . The natural question now arises . . . why is there a delay in disclosing to the public just what the Harrison, Ballard, and Allen plan is? [It] would seem wise to present the zoning proposals without further delay.[21]

But on August 16, Mayor O'Dwyer announced that he was resigning as mayor to become ambassador to Mexico.[22] The mayor's resignation was to have direct consequence for the Harrison, Ballard, and Allen (hereafter referred to as HB&A) plan. A special election was held to fill the vacated mayoralty. Vincent Impellitteri, president of the Council, was acting mayor and aspired to keep the position he was filling. The Regular Democratic organization had other ideas, however, and nominated Ferdinand Pecora after a bruising contest. The Republicans, hoping to capitalize on the dissension in the Democratic ranks, nominated Edward Corsi. Impellitteri refused to be counted out of the race, however. He ran as an Independent.

The campaign was hard-fought and confused—charges, recriminations, and complex maneuvering characterized the struggle.[23] Finkelstein, a Regular Democrat, publicly gave his support to Pecora (Moses, incidentally, supported Impellitteri). Impellitteri won. In November he announced that Finkelstein would be replaced as chairman of the Planning Commission.[24]

During the campaign, moreover, Impellitteri had refused to call a meeting of the Board of Estimate to appropriate the necessary money to publish the HB&A report, relying on various devices to fend off Finkelsetin's public pleas for publication.[25] On October 26 the Board of Estimate did vote to authorize the printing and publication of 2,000 copies of the plan—too late for it to be mailed before the election. The board, under Impellitteri's prompting, also insisted that each copy of the consultants' report carry a statement that the Board of Estimate was in no way committed to the contents of the proposal.[26]

On December 14, 1950, Impellitteri announced that John J. Bennett, chief justice of the Court of Special Sessions, would succeed Finkelstein. Bennett, with a background in law and Brooklyn Democratic politics, had worked closely with Robert Moses on a number of projects, and his relations with both Moses and Impellitteri were sympathetic and cordial.[27]

Five months after Bennett became chairman of the Planning Commission, the Harrison, Ballard, and Allen proposal made its debut. On April 29, 1951, the consultants' report was released to the press and copies forwarded to "interested" groups and individuals.

The HB&A report proposed to limit the future population capacity of the city to approximately twelve million people, as compared with the fifty-five million that the 1916 Resolution permitted. This was to be achieved through reduction of residential building bulk. The text of the proposal made a borough-by-borough summary. Except for Manhattan, bulk was to be cut back—in Queens, Brooklyn, and Staten Island sharply so. In Manhattan, the report proposed to "sort out existing patterns" of land uses chiefly through its new administrative provisions.

In its administrative sections the report asked for a reduction of the discretionary powers of the Board of Standards and Appeals. It then went on to refer to the problem of nonconforming uses and said, "It is proposed to require the elimination of certain objectionable uses . . . after an appropriate period of amortization."[28]

Two days after the release of the plan, the New York (Manhattan) Chapter of the AIA released a report itself, in which it said that the new plan was "sound" and "flexible and adaptable."[29] Even with this encouragement the Planning Commission took no further action on the plan.

In November, 1951, the Citizens Union issued an enthusiastic report on the HB&A proposal: "It [the proposal] will constitute, in our judgment, one of the most important improvements ever made in the government of New York City."[30] The Citizens Union went on to urge the Planning Commission to change the proposal in the direction of stricter bulk controls, if any changes were to be made.

Time continued to pass without action from the Planning Commission, however. On December 30, 1951, the New York Chamber of Commerce expressed approval of the plan's general approach and asked for public hearings to be held.[31]

It became increasingly clear that the Planning Commission had no intention of pressing the issue to an early conclusion. This seems to have been in part due to the community of interest between Bennett and Moses, a community of interest that did not include zoning revision. Bennett, moreover, had succumbed to the siren call of master planning—elaborate population studies were being conducted that absorbed the attention and time of the staff.[32] As one staff member said,

There was no push from the top and the staff was too busy with other things. . . . No one was really out in the field rounding up interest and support for the proposal. Somehow the original push was lost.

There was a mounting impatience with the failure of the commission to bring the plan to hearings, however. The Citizens Union and the Commerce and Industry Association called for action. Finally, almost a year after the release of the plan, the Planning Commission scheduled the first round of hearings to begin on March 25, 1952. This decision was made over the objections of the Metropolitan Real Estate Boards

Association (an association whose members were representatives from each of the five borough real estate boards, hereafter referred to as the MREBA). The MREBA asked for more time to study the proposals.[33] It was already annoyed. Although the consultant firm claimed it had conferred with the major realtors in the city, the borough real estate boards felt that they had been omitted from the process of formulating the proposals.[34]

The first hearing, on March 25, 1952, lasted six hours with thirty-three speakers.[35] Only one group, the Twenty-third Street Association, went on record as being in opposition. Support came primarily from the "good government" groups— the Regional Plan Association, the Citizens Union, and the City Club. The Citizens Budget Commission "generally endorsed" the proposal. The Brooklyn and the New York Real Estate Boards, the Fifth Avenue Association, and the Commerce and Industry Association asked for more time for study. The hearings wore on through April,[36] and the pattern remained constant. The major Reform-oriented groups praised the plan and occasionally asked that it be more restrictive; the real estate and business groups asked for more time.

Shortly after the conclusion of the hearings, the MREBA issued a report on the proposal.[37] The report was the work of a joint committee of representatives from each of the borough real estate boards, but the main task had been performed by Latham Squire, architect, engineer, and consultant to the New York Real Estate Board.[38] The report began by admitting that "the present Resolution is outdated and inadequate—this applies to the Zoning Maps as well as the text of the Resolution. Both the text and the maps are greatly in need of modernization."[39] The report then launched into a criticism of the bulk controls (a "considerable amount . . . of adjustment will be necessary") and the nonconforming use provision ("all of which are probably legally unsound, unenforceable, and not desirable"). The report granted that a few of the proposals had merit, but the opinion of the real estate boards, as expressed by the report, was clearly hostile to the basic provisions of the plan.

At the same time, the MREBA Committee turned to other sources for help. Squire had been holding frequent luncheon meetings with Harris Murdock, chairman of the Board of Standards and Appeals. The report reflected the outcome of these meetings; it contained a sharp attack on lessening the discretion or jurisdiction of the BSA. Squire had also consulted with Wagner, who was borough president of Manhattan and a leading candidate for mayor for the 1953 elections, but apparently with less success. Wagner had, after all, initiated the rezoning effort and had a commitment to planning.

Squire also turned for assistance to Dowling's Citizens Zoning Committee. The CZC was nearly defunct,[40] and Dowling was not enthusiastic. He had sold many of his large real estate holdings, and the effort of maintaining the CZC was more trouble than it seemed to be worth. Squire continued to press for cooperation, however.

The Planning Commission suspended further hearings until the fall. When the hearings were reopened on November 7, 1952, the MREBA offered the Planning Commission a counterproposal. Squire suggested that the 1916 Resolution be amended rather than rewritten. Commissioner Orton, who acted as liaison officer between the Planning Commission and the consultants, answered angrily, "You could no more do that than you could put a jet engine and hydraulic drive into a Model T Ford." [41] Squire then asked the Planning Commission to hold a special hearing on the MREBA report. The Planning Commission refused to commit itself, but neither did it call for a vote on the rezoning proposal.

The real estate boards were clearly willing to see the Zoning Resolution amended, but they wanted assurance that the amendments were moderate and incremental rather than a sweeping revision such as the consultants suggested. Orton, speaking for the commission, was unwilling to make as substantial a concession as Squire sought, however, and the MREBA and the Planning Commission were unable to find any basis for negotiation.

Squire's effort to rejuvenate the Citizens Zoning Committee was successful. On December 17, 1952, the CZC announced it's formal reappearance. Dowling accepted a lesser post (treasurer) than he had previously held, and Henry J. Davenport, president of the New York Real Estate Board, became chairman of the CZC. Squire was named consultant to the committee.[42]

On December 20 Orton reenunciated his commitment to comprehensive rezoning in a letter to the New York *Times*.[43] This letter was primarily a repetition of the arguments he had made in the public hearings and underscored the commission's unwillingness to negotiate on the principle of rezoning.

The Planning Commission reopened hearings on the proposal on January 12, 1953, on a borough-by-borough basis. The first hearing, in Manhattan, evidenced a sharp division of interests. Most groups aligned for or against the plan in accordance with their local interests, with a bare numerical majority opposing the plan.[44] The New York Real Estate Board repeated its opposition to the consultants' proposal, and once again Squire offered a counterproposal. Squire's suggestion was for the Planning Commission, representatives of the borough presidents, the commissioner of buildings, and members of the real estate boards to form into a commission to restudy the 1916 Resolution and make proposals independent of the work of HB&A. The Planning Commission ignored this suggestion. The issue was thus effectively drawn as a conflict of principle between the HB&A proposals and the views of the real estate boards.

On March 2 the Planning Commission held its hearings in

Brooklyn. Frank Barrera, for the Brooklyn Real Estate Board, argued that the changes, especially the bulk reductions, were "too drastic." The Brooklyn Chamber of Commerce asked for more space for industry. The homeowners' groups asked for increased protection from apartment houses, retail activities, and industry.

The pattern was repeated in Queens. Homeowners were willing to favor the proposal, although they invariably asked for more protection for their areas. The retail, real estate, and industry groups requested more space and less restrictive bulk provisions, and expressed resentment at proposed upgrading of unrestricted or commercial zones. In the Bronx, the first public opposition from a member of the Board of Estimate appeared. Lyons, Bronx borough president, flatly stated that the plan was unrealistic, too complicated, and would be harmful to the city and his borough. The Bronx Board of Trade, Real Estate Board, and Chamber of Commerce supported the views of Lyons. The opposition, moreover, relied heavily on the arguments (and even the wording) of the MREBA report, and Latham Squire was present at the hearing, acting for the CZC.[45]

In Staten Island, Borough President Edward G. Baker opposed the proposal on June 15. This concluded the second round of hearings, and there was little to cheer the proponents of the revisions. Two borough presidents openly opposed the plan, and they were joined by an impressive array of economic interest groups. There was support, but even this was qualified. The Regional Plan Association, the Citizens Union, and the City Club agreed with the proposals, but they were agitating for more restrictive provisions. There was, moreover, opposition of a less public nature. The Board of Standards and Appeals was unhappy with the consultants' recommendations, and Moses had, on numerous occasions, made himself clear in his objection to the plan. While it is difficult to measure

Moses' influence on Bennett and Impellitteri, Moses maintained friendly and sympathetic relations with them.

Nor was the commission staff used effectively to promote
the plan. Elements of the staff were physically separated and
had been since the inception of the Planning Commission.[46]
Further,

there was no real effort to coordinate its [the staff's] work. Some
would be working on zoning, some on master planning population
studies, some on details. For the HB&A proposal, no one really
tried to pull the staff together, to get this fellow or that to drop
his pet—although perfectly legitimate—interest and do something to
rustle up support or to find a basis for agreement.

Although many of the civic associations gave support, the
Planning Commission made no effort to articulate this support
and to bring it to bear in a concentrated fashion. In August,
1953, the Citizens Union reported "an increasing restlessness
among our membership about the long delays in comprehensive rezoning."[47] The Citizens Budget Commission, not
strongly committed to the HB&A proposals but willing to see
rezoning, said:

The City Planning Commission shows a commendable caution,
greatly overdone; a degree of imagination, also commendable, but
wholly inadequate; and a degree and kind of leadership which
generates useful debate but results in no decision.[48]

This was the requiem for the Harrison, Ballard, and Allen
proposal. Although the City Club and the Citizens Union
attempted to revive the plan in the next two years, the Planning Commission never held further hearings or a vote on the
proposal. The commission had been defeated by a strongly
organized resistance and its own unwillingness to do battle for
the HB&A plan.

The Wagner Era: 1953–1960 [49]

During the 1950s, building activity continued in New York
City.[50] Despite predictions to the contrary, the city's land econ-

omy staved off the threat of stagnation or retardation. Although
Manhattan steadily lost population, this loss was overcome by
increased commercial building (which may, in fact, have the
effect of forcing residents out), while Staten Island, Queens,
and Brooklyn had population increases.[51] The skyscraper
(whose demise had long been anticipated) staged a resurgence,
and Manhattan especially bristled with rising steel girders.

At the same time, the city's politics continued to change. In
1953 Wagner successfully stood for the mayoralty on the Democratic ticket, as he did in 1957 (and, for that matter, again in
1961). In the years following 1953, he was often accused of
belonging to the "bosses," of abandoning his political friends
to join the Reformers, of being weak, indecisive, or at best
indifferent to the real interests of the city—depending on one's
political predispositions. Wagner nevertheless rose to the final
test of political success: continued survival in a dangerous and
competitive environment.

As the decade progressed, the Reformers became increasingly
active. The "Reform cycle" of the 1950s was different from
earlier efforts, however. Unlike the movements that carried
Mitchel and La Guardia to the mayor's office, the Reformers
of the 1950s attempted not "Fusion" (that is, a wedding of the
local Republicans with the dissatisfied middle-class elements
of the Democrats) but to win control of the Regular Democratic party organization.[52] Wagner, as mayor and titular
Democratic party chieftain, was able to take advantage of the
conflict between Reformers and Regulars and came near con-
verting the title to reality.

He rarely pleased both Regular and Reformer but he preserved a degree of cohesion to strengthen his own position.[53]

Although the Reform Democrats had only limited interest
in comprehensive zoning per se, their activities set the stage
for a rezoning effort. The interests of the Reformer—a concern
with the city as a whole, with grass-roots democracy, with

efficient and honest government, and with governmental foresight and rational approaches to the problems of urbanization[54] —were entirely compatible with the goals of planning and the ideology of comprehensive zoning. It was likely that the more that Wagner came to depend on the Reform Democrats for political support, the more benefit he would find in endorsing a program such as comprehensive zoning.

The Planning Commission—the weapon for implementing comprehensive zoning—was in an unenviable position, however. Consistently beaten on its zoning proposals, completely ineffectual in its other Charter-mandated duties, the commission was having difficulty keeping the thin shreds of prestige that remained to it. In a changing city, the Planning Commission seemed unable to control its own activities, much less impose a guiding hand on the physical development of the city.

The harsh humiliation of the HB&A plan had some beneficent side effects for the Planning Commission, however, Wagner, as chairman of the commission, had initiated the effort and he apparently carried his commitment to comprehensive zoning to the mayor's office. Further, HB&A had donated some of its staff members to the Planning Commission. Competent professionals, they had been schooled in the complexities of New York City zoning politics by their experience with the 1949–53 effort.

Voorhees, Walker, Smith, and Smith: First Phase

Late in 1955, Chairman Bennett announced his retirement, giving Mayor Wagner his first chance to make an appointment to the Planning Commission. The mayor appointed James Felt (at that time directing the affairs of the Real Estate Bureau) as the new chairman. Felt was an almost ideal appointment. The son of a realtor, he had augmented his father's fortune and was one of the most successful realtors in the city.[55] He was deeply respected within his own competitive fraternity. Of great personal charm and persuasiveness, he preferred to deal on a face-to-face basis (where his personal attributes were most effective). He had strong convictions and, once adopting a position, fought intensely for what he believed right. As one of his opponents said:

The thing about Jack Felt is that, even if you disagree with his ideas, you have to acknowledge that he is doing what he is doing in complete honesty and with complete integrity. And, if you're trying to oppose him, watch yourself when you talk to him personally, because in five minutes flat he'll convince you that you're wrong and he is right just through his personal qualities.

It was clear that Felt saw zoning revision as the first order of priority for the Planning Commission. Shortly after taking office on January 1, 1956, Felt announced that "rezoning is a must" for the city.[56]

Chairman Felt turned to rezoning because it was the most concrete hope of the Planning Commission. Master planning as such was ineffective, and the same was true of capital budget programming. The commission was sadly in need of a real accomplishment. A Planning Commission staff member said Felt saw the probelm as

one of building some basis for the commission—a friendly constituency and a record of success in at least one of its Charter areas. Although he saw zoning as necessary and important in itself, he thought it was even more important for the commission to win at something and to find a constituency.

For James Felt the issue was one of survival of the Planning Commission. Perhaps it was not a question of survival of existence (it seemed unlikely that after twenty years the Planning Commission would follow Walker's City Planning Board to oblivion) but it was certainly a matter of survival of function.

As first steps toward improving the status of the commission, Felt requested appropriations for staff increases, the recruitment necessary to fill staff vacancies, and the means to bring the commission and staff under one roof. In all three areas he was successful.[57]

On July 22, 1956, Felt announced his intention to undertake a new study of the city's zoning. He said that the study would be carried through to a revision of the existing resolution "if it was the last thing" he accomplished while in office.[58] The procedure was to be that used for the HB&A study—consultants would be hired to do the necessary research and prepare the proposal.

On August 30, 1956, a request for $150,000 to retain the architectural firm of Voorhees, Walker, Smith, and Smith (hereafter referred to as VWS&S) went to the Board of Estimate. That same day, in spite of a dissenting vote by Bronx Borough President Lyons, the Board of Estimate granted the appropriation.[59]

The task, for the next two and a half years, was turned over to the consultants.[60] In the interlude between the hiring of VWS&S and the public unveiling of the plan, the commission, staff, and consultants worked closely together, but within limits. Felt intended to rely on a strategy of "consultantship," that is, any proposal from VWS&S could be, if fiercely opposed, disclaimed or bargained by the Planning Commission without openly admitting defeat. Accordingly, a good part of the consultants' work was done in near secrecy and ostensibly apart from the routine of the Planning Commission.

Decisions of timing had to be made. The press, at least, had attributed the failure of the HB&A plan to the confusion of issues involved in the 1950 election, since Bennett and Impellitteri brought a lack of enthusiasm to a project that had been advocated by a political opponent. Should the VWS&S proposal be released for hearings and debate before the 1961 elections? Too long a delay might suggest a lack of drive and interest from the Planning Commission and the mayor. On the other

hand, a defeat on zoning before the election would not
strengthen the mayor's position with the Reformers; still, a
victory would be a concrete "step forward" that the mayor
could point to with pride. It was decided to press the issue to
an early conclusion. A defeat could be repaired or at least
blamed on the mayor's political opponents. Delay might carry
the more onerous burden of seeming to be vacillation or
indifference.[61]

Three years after Felt publicly announced that the commission was to undertake a zoning study, the consultants released
their results. On February 16, 1959, the VWS&S proposal, entitled *Rezoning New York City,* was distributed to the press
and more general distribution began.

The VWS&S plan resembled the Harrison, Ballard, and
Allen proposal of eight years before, but it was more restrictive
than the earlier plan. Where the HB&A plan had called for a
maximum population of 12,619,000, the VWS&S plan zoned
the city for a maximum of 10,940,000 (as contrasted with the
permitted 55,000,000 inhabitants under the existing zoning).
VWS&S recommended even greater bulk cutbacks than had
been advised in 1951. The VWS&S proposal introduced a concept new to New York: "performance standards" for industry.[62]

The use districts were renamed and redescribed and, in
some cases, had their boundaries radically adjusted. As with
the HB&A proposal, the greatest adjustment of use district
boundaries was in Queens and Staten Island, where the
patterns of land use were not already set.

In its administrative sections, the VWS&S plan returned to
nonconforming uses and, like the HB&A proposal, specified
their elimination. Further, the new plan recommended that a
zoning administrator be established under the Department of
Buildings and that many of the existing functions of the Board
of Standards and Appeals be transferred to such an officer.

The proposal was lengthy and complex, and the commission

members recognized that their first task was explanation and clarification of the plan, since many groups might oppose it simply because it was difficult to understand.

It was perhaps a mistake to introduce so much new vocabulary [a planner said]. A lot of groups, especially homeowners, small business groups, and real estate groups, are wary of confusing innovations—changes that might have a hidden or legalistic kicker in them.

By February 19 the Planning Commission had mailed letters to 300 groups and established a schedule for mailing 2,000 copies of the plan along with explanatory brochures.[63] By March 2—two weeks after the plan's release—Felt had set four members of the staff to the full-time task of answering queries on the proposal.[64]

The early reactions in February were encouraging to the Planning Commission. The New York Chapter of the AIA cautiously endorsed the proposal, largely for its increased "flexibility" in bulk regulations.[65] On February 21 Queens Borough President Clancy met with Felt to discuss the plan. Clancy, after the interview, generally endorsed the proposal and suggested that the limitations on the Board of Standards and Appeals might be wise.[66]

On February 22 Felt appeared on television to answer questions about the proposal and to recruit supporters. When asked about the mayor's views, Felt replied, "The Mayor is very anxious to see that a new, modern zoning resolution is put into effect." [67] Felt was careful not to say that the mayor supported the consultants' proposal, however. When asked about Moses' reactions, Felt answered that Moses "will probably—and I say this hopefully—endorse the resolution in principle." [68] He concluded the interview with a pledge to fight for zoning revision.

In the following weeks, additional signs of endorsement appeared. The Citizens Union approved the plan with the reservation that it would study the plan further.[69] By March 9, 1959, the Planning Commission could claim to have received "more than 100" letters, "most of them expressing approval." [70]

There were undercurrents of opposition, however. These were still discrete and only half-expressed. Builders and realtors began to show a sensitivity to the plan. They were especially worried that the proposals might introduce uncertainty and instability in the land market.[71] Felt moved to scotch some of the doubts. On March 30, 1959, he announced that the consultants had been asked to insert a "grace period" in the proposal that would delay enforcement for a year or eighteen months after the final enactment.[72] He said that the grace period was for the benefit of the builders and that he was committed to having it in the proposal. The concession was a shrewed political tactic. In effect Felt was saying that the Planning Commission had the interests of the builders at heart and that the commission was attempting to safeguard these interests.

The grace period was not popular with the planning staff, however. They saw it as an abdication of the function of zoning. Reform-oriented interest groups reacted the same way.[73]

During the first week of April, the Metropolitan Real Estate Boards Association appointed a committee to study the proposal. The composition of the committee differed little from that of its counterpart appointed in 1950. Frank Barrera was chairman, and Latham Squire was once again the consultant. As with the earlier committee, this one focused on the main body of the proposal, while specific objections were left with the individual borough real estate boards. There was no reason to believe that the newer committee would be more friendly to the 1959 proposal than they had been to the HB&A plan: the provisions which had excited the wrath of these same men were in the VWS&S proposal.

The Planning Commission set the first "informal" hearing for April 13, 1959. On April 12 the borough president of Manhattan, Hulan Jack, announced that he was "unequivocally opposed" to the new plan.[74] Jack's opposition was well timed. As one of those who would vote on the resolution (if it ever came to the Board of Estimate) and as president of Manhattan, he very early threw a cloud over the Planning Commission's effort. The same day, however, the Citizens Budget Commission gave its support without reservations.[75] Thus the consultants' proposal was entering its first test of strength in a mixed atmosphere.

The informal hearings did little to clear the air.[76] On April 13 and 14 the commission held hearings on the proposal in general. Forty-eight organizations were represented. The list of those offering support was impressive: the City Club, the Citizens Budget Commission, the Citizens Union, the Womens City Club, and the Citizens Housing and Planning Council were only a few of the thirty-one groups specifically favoring the revisions. The New York Building Congress also approved the proposal, with the addition of the grace period. The giant Federation of Queens Civic Councils, although unable to speak officially for its member organizations, gave support with the qualification that certain amendments might be needed.

There were only eight groups that were wholly or almost wholly critical of the proposal. Some of these were groups who saw a familiar threat in the nonconforming use provisions.[77] The United Builders Association, fearing that the proposal might inhibit future building activity, opposed the plan. The Staten Island Home Builders Association, worried by the decreased bulk allowances for the Island, was also critical. And the Fifth Avenue Association threw its prestigious name against the plan; the association feared that the avenue was not getting the special consideration it merited. The real estate boards were silent.

Two weeks later, on April 27, hearings were held on the provisions for the Bronx. The Bronx Chamber of Commerce and the Bronx Real Estate Board, which were acting jointly, took a "wait and see" attitude. In general, the homeowners' groups were enthusiastic over the proposal. Where these organizations showed doubt it was from a fear that their areas were insufficiently protected. The builders' groups, conversely, were unhappy. They felt that the proposed bulk regulations were too stringent, that too much land was being given to residential uses and not enough to "future development" (presumably of high-rise buildings, industry, and commercial activities).

This was to be the pattern for the hearings held in Queens, Staten Island, Manhattan, and Brooklyn during the first three weeks of May, 1959. The real estate boards waited for the report of the MREBA, the homeowners' organizations focused on the specific problems of their areas, and the business groups tended to ask for protection and expansion of their local "jurisdictions."

At the same time, the delicate task of negotiation began. Throughout the hearings Felt relied on "consultantship"; when faced with strong opposition he reacted characteristically as follows:

Building Industry League Representative: You can't legislate ways of life. . . . Some things zoning can't do. We are worried about your too fast action, it is a big document. . . . Now, first, the 100 foot by 100 plot is out. The regulation would require reassemblage. . . .

Chairman Felt: We'll meet with you on the specific potentialities of the 100 by 100 plot in different districts. . . . This is the consultants' proposal and we'll listen to what all groups have to suggest. We endorse the proposal in principle, but we may have to make many changes.

Building Industry League: We deeply appreciate your attitude, sir.[78]

The commission attempted to preserve a public air of neutrality toward the proposal (after all, it was not their proposal) and to bring opposing or doubtful groups in for "conferences." By the time of the Manhattan hearings, for example, the Fifth Avenue Association's doubts had been partly assuaged. The association conferred at length with members of the Planning Commission and was gradually being convinced that there was room for modification of the proposal favorable to the association's desires.

But the seeds of opposition continued to grow. Some builders' groups and the real estate organizations either withheld support or delivered attacks on the plan. In Staten Island, the Chamber of Commerce and the Real Estate Boards were working together on a joint committee and were trying to increase the number of their allies. In the Bronx, the Real Estate Board and the Board of Trade were allied. The Brooklyn Downtown Civic Association (a business group) was "cooperating" with the Brooklyn Real Estate Board on the MREBA study.[79] For the Planning Commission, the obvious danger was that these elements might be brought together in a solid and possibly impregnable front of organized resistance.

With the conclusion of the informal hearings, the Planning Commission and its staff turned to preventing a solid bloc of opposition. The late spring and summer of 1959 saw the commission offices become a hive of activity. As a first step, on May 7, 1959, Robert Dowling announced that the Citizens Committee for Modern Zoning (hereafter referred to as the CMZ) had been formed.[80] The CMZ, which had been in preparation for some time, did "not intend to let this issue die as has happened so often in the past." [81] Although Dowling had led the opposition against the Moses plan in 1944–45 and had been an active opponent of the HB&A plan, he was to be co-chairman of the CMZ with Luther Gulick. Dowling, whatever his earlier reactions to comprehensive zoning, admired James Felt and considered Felt a close and affectionate friend. Dowling was more than willing to contribute his time and influence to advocating a proposal that Felt saw as important. Gulick was a political scientist, the first City Administrator (in 1953), Re-

form-oriented, and head of the Institute of Public Administration.

The Committee for Modern Zoning grew out of discussions
by Gulick, Felt, and members of the Planning Commission
staff. Felt apparently had taken the initiative in the idea, although quietly. The purpose of the CMZ was to provide the
same service the 1913 and 1914 Zoning Commissions had. It
would supply an informal channel to the financial and business
communities of the city and provide a means for the Planning
Commission to advocate its position through the mouths of
others. A planner commented:

> There were certain kinds of stands, certain arguments that the
> commission could not take itself. With access to the "inner circles"
> of lots of interests and groups, it was possible to put certain views
> in the right ears without seeming to push. . . . It was a way of
> getting certain influential types involved—men whose voices would
> be listened to if you could convince them to speak, and by putting
> a man's name on a letterhead you give him a psychological commit-
> ment to what that letterhead represents.
>
> Simply, many realtors could be persuaded by David Rockefeller,
> Tishman, Dowling, so forth, in a way that they could not be
> persuaded by the Planning Commission staff. And the same was
> true of the big builders.

The commission staff began to take action on the objections
voiced in the hearings. The first task of the staff was to contact
local groups who were frightened or confused by the novelty
of the proposal and to "educate" them out of their doubts. The
second task was more difficult. The commission had to find a
basis on which to present its own proposal. At some point, Felt
would have to offer a plan for which the commission was
willing to fight, a plan which was the commission's and not
"just the consultants'." To prepare for this, the commission staff
had to sort through the objections and criticisms, decide which
were valid, which were bargainable, and which could be
safely ignored.

As far as the potential opposition was concerned, the

MREBA, led by Barrera, was preparing its report. Work proceeded slowly, however. Latham Squire, who had been the backbone of the opposition to the HB&A plan, was ill—mortally so, as it developed. Physically unable to use his vast range of skills and contacts, he could not provide the expertise to muster an organized attack on the proposal. Then, on May 10, 1959, Harris Murdock, chairman of the BSA, died. Although the Board of Standards and Appeals continued its friendly relations with builders, architects, and realtors, Murdock had handled virtually all of the business of the BSA for nearly thirty years, and the relations between the BSA and its constituents had been formed and set by him. As a source of opposition from within the government, the BSA was weakened by Murdock's death. As a mustering point for opposing building and real estate groups, it was temporarily out of the fight.[82] These two chance events, in combination with the natural divisive forces within the interest group population, made the strategic problem of organizing resistance difficult.

The Second Phase

On June 24, 1959, the Planning Commission announced that it was incorporating a one-year grace period (from the time of passage) into the rezoning proposal. This was the commission's first step toward presenting its own, more relaxed, and more "realistic" proposal.[83] The addition of the grace period was greeted by the CMZ as evidence of the "cooperative" stance that Felt was taking, and it provided the CMZ with valuable material for seeking support for the proposal among builders and realtors.[84]

Late in the fall of 1959, the commission allowed little driblets of its revised plan to leak out: a plan which would be more relaxed than that offered by the consultants, and one for which the commission was willing to fight. At the same time, the Metropolitan Association of Real Estate Boards was preparing its final report. But the MREBA was caught in an awkward position. Depending on the degree of revision of the original proposal, its critique might be obsolete almost before it was released; yet if it waited for the revised version, the MREBA would have to begin its study anew. Its hope was to gain the initiative in its report, but the effect might be dissipated if the Planning Commission had anticipated too many of its objections.

On November 30, 1959, the MREBA report was released. It largely repeated the protests that the earlier critique of the HB&A plan had contained: Why scrap a working, ongoing system for one that was novel and unknown? Bulk cuts were too drastic; "it would be economically impossible to construct new buildings in most instances"; the "performance standards have no place in a zoning resolution."

The nonconforming use requirements were singled out for special attack, and on now-familiar grounds; they were described as "arbitrary" and "inflexible," and the report condemned the provisions without qualification. It also attacked the idea of a zoning administrator. "The provisions . . .[on the office and powers of the zoning administrator] are highly objectionable and unnecessary." [85]

With the release of the report, Frank Barrera, the youthful and talented counsel for the Brooklyn Real Estate Board who had inherited Squire's mantle, held a press interview. He attacked the VWS&S proposal in strong terms; it "would deal a most damaging blow to the future of New York." [86] The "proposal is fundamentally wrong" and it "lays down strict rules for land usage that would do credit to an authoritarian government." [87] Barrera opposed "drastic and wholesale" change instead of making a district-by-district amendment of the old plan.

But on December 1, Felt replied to Barrera's objections. He stated simply that the amended version, which would soon be released by the commission, would remove many of the grounds for objection that Barrera had expressed.[88] And on December 11, 1959, the revised plan was made public. In the December revision, the position of zoning administrator was dropped. In important and rapidly changing areas of Manhattan, especially areas that were shifting to higher-rent housing, bulk restrictions were relaxed.[89] (Felt commented that these relaxations were very "likely to win the support of many real estate groups.") [90] Bulk restrictions for the city as a whole, except for Staten Island, were generally relaxed. Under the original plan, the allowable population would have been approximately eleven million; under the December revision, nearly one million more. The number of districts for industry were increased, and the promised grace period appeared. Moreover, of 723 requests for map changes received during or after the hearings, 366 had been granted. A large proportion of these changes went to homeowners' organizations (105 had been granted to Queens groups).[91]

Felt said that he intended to "fight relentlessly" for the revised plan.[92] There were other important aspects to the changes, however. The Planning Commission had shown a willingness to bargain across the board—with industry, real estate, builders, and homeowners. Besides undercutting many of the MREBA's objections, there was the implicit promise of room for more negotiation: on nonconforming uses, mapping adjustments, further bulk reductions, parking provisions, and on the industrial performance standards.

The December revision marked a turning point in the struggle. The Planning Commission could no longer claim it was merely discussing a proposal offered by "outside" consultants; the commission itself was committed to a proposal—and to winning or losing.

At this point Felt and members of the staff and commission began to plan and pursue a self-conscious strategy to win. Their problems were multifaceted. Few groups had given a total commitment of support. The New York Chapter of the AIA was sympathetic, but the Architects Council (of which the New York Chapter of AIA was a member) was definitely hostile and was fighting hard to keep its largest constituent group in line. Although there was some restlessness among the membership of the real estate groups, officially at least the total membership of the MREBA was opposed to the plan. While the New York Building Congress had early given its support, the Building Industry League and most of the borough or local building groups were still in opposition. Many of the local business associations were either uncommitted or showing hostility. And although the homeowners were gradually being won over, this was a slow and painful process.

Felt and his aides formulated a two-pronged attack. The first effort would be to break the will of the opposition. They accepted as given the divided nature of the opposition and decided to concentrate on preserving this state of affairs. Through bargaining, through Felt's persuasiveness and contacts in the building and real estate communities, and through the quiet work of the CMZ, the commission hoped to isolate their opponents and then pick them off one by one. The second effort would be aimed at creating a "ground swell of grass-roots" support. This "grass-roots" effort could be achieved only by the staff working in the field, persuading, propogandizing, bargaining, and educating. The aim was to create a climate in which the members of the Board of Estimate would be confronted with such widespread support for the plan that they could not consider it politically safe to cast a negative vote on the proposal.

It would not be easy to convince the members of the Board of Estimate that it would be unwise to vote against the proposal. Bronx Borough President Lyons had lost none of his distaste for the Planning Commission and zoning. He could (perhaps) be forced to respond to "overwhelming popular" support of the revision. Clancy, Queens borough president, was showing a favorable disposition toward the proposal, but it would be necessary to continue building up pressure through the Queens homeowners' groups to ensure his affirmative vote. The Brooklyn borough president, Cashmore, was not personally in favor of rezoning, but, like Lyons, it might be possible to generate enough support to force his vote. Hulan Jack, Manhattan borough president, had already opposed the consultants' plan; could he be persuaded the revised version was less objectionable? Staten Island Borough President Maniscalco was privately committed to rezoning for the Island, in spite of the dogged opposition of the Staten Island Real Estate Board, Chamber of Commerce, and Board of Trade alliance.

Of the three city-wide officers on the Board of Estimate the mayor was committed to rezoning. But the mayor had given Felt reason to think that he was unwilling to go to a sharply divided Board of Estimate with a rezoning proposal. The mayor had given much time and energy to trying to strengthen his position on the board—he did not want to enter a full-scale battle with the borough presidents over rezoning. The comptroller and the president of the Council would probably react in the same manner as the mayor. If support for the proposal was general and strong, the city-wide officers would vote favorably.

For the Planning Commission and its staff, the margin of error often seemed tenuous:

It was touchy work. We could never be sure. . . . So-and-so would start reading his copy of the proposal and run across something he had not seen before. The next thing we knew the phone would ring and he would want to know what the hell we were trying to put over on his people. So then we would explain and cajole and sooth his feathers, only it might happen all over again the next day.

The beginning of 1960 presented the opponents of the proposal with an even cloudier field than it did the Planning Commission. There were some strong centers of opposition— among them the real estate and business groups in Staten Island, the Queens Chamber of Commerce, and the Brooklyn and Bronx Real Estate Boards. The Architects Council (including the borough chapters of the American Institute of Architects) was hostile to the proposal. The builders' groups were divided, however. Further, communication among all these groups was low. The MREBA report had failed as a rallying point for the opposition. Local concerns and group autonomy tended toward separateness of action. Moreover, the intensive campaigning of the planners and their allies was eroding the bases for opposition. For example, one realtor said:

Many realtors began to agree with Felt, because they liked him, because they respected his opinions and his integrity. Some might have had doubts, but they were willing to listen and play along until they were solidly convinced he was wrong, and this rarely happened. He never let the issue die; he never let [the opposition] get and keep anyone's ear for long. Even though many realtors were not willing to say so publicly at first, a lot of builders and realtors were privately in favor of the resolution and just waiting the chance to say so.

Although Barrera made efforts to rally the opposition, his staff aid was small—there were only about five men working to promote opposition—and the prevailing attitude was to allow the local groups to handle their local problems. Members of the MREBA Committee gave talks in the boroughs, but these were few in number when compared to the effort that the Planning Commission and its staff was making.[93]

The next public test came in March and April, 1960, when the Planning Commission had scheduled formal public hearings on the revised plan. As the date of the first hearing neared, activity intensified. At a meeting of the New York Real Estate Board, on February 11, Felt and Barrera confronted each other face to face. The debate was heated. Barrera attempted to show that the proposed resolution would hamper building, reduce land values, and generally have debilitating effect on the future of the city.[94] Felt counterattacked as sharply; he pooh-poohed Barrera's claims as "inaccurate" and as misrepresentations of the provisions of the code. And on February 15, in the pages of the New York *Journal-American,* a letter appeared from Robert Moses. It was ambiguous, but it seemed to say that the proposed resolution had little of value to offer.[95] The risk was apparent and real. Moses had been silent to date, but his opposition to the code would be critical, and there was little reason to believe that the man who had opposed the HB&A plan would be favorably disposed toward the new proposal. Felt moved quietly to win Moses' support or at least to neutralize him.

On March 14, 1960, the public hearings began. Felt opened the first meeting by saying, "We shall reject any counsel of delay or postponement." He went on to say, "In deference to the genuine problems of the professionals in real estate and building we have proposed a year's grace period." [96] And the procession of speakers began.

As the hearings unfolded, it was increasingly clear that the careful groundwork of the planning staff was having results. Twenty speakers favored the proposal and, while many had details to quibble about (especially the homeowners' groups), the number of those favoring the resolution must have been a comfort to the Planning Commission. The City Club, the New York (County) Bar Association, the Citizens Housing and Planning Council, the Municipal Art Society, the Federation of Civic Councils of Queens (many of its constituent groups spoke independently), and the Citizens Budget Commission were loud in their praises. Ten groups appeared on the first day to oppose the proposal. The Metropolitan Real Estate Boards Association, the Building Industry League, the Avenue of Americas Association, and the Architects Council were the major groups standing in opposition.

During the hearings, Felt worked to cultivate an atmosphere

of cooperation. He asked the speaker from the Avenue of the Americas Association to come to see him, adding, "You and I have been on intimate terms for years now." [97] And Felt worked hard to underscore the divisions in the opposition. When Max Simon rose to speak for the Architects Council, Felt asked him if the architects who had spoken in favor of the code were members of the council. Simon was forced to admit that they were.[98] And when another architect rose to speak, Felt was careful to lead him to point out that he was a member of the New York Chapter of the AIA Zoning Committee and a member of the Zoning Committee of the Architects Council, and that he was dissenting from Max Simon's views. The speaker for the City Club asked: If David Tishman favors the proposal, if David Rockefeller favors the proposal, if Robert Dowling favors the proposal (all members of the CMZ), could Barrera be speaking for the real estate community?

Max Koenig, speaking for the Building Industry League, pointed out that "there was no original consultation with informed groups of these categories [builders, architects, and engineers] to seek mutual understanding and assistance." [99]

Frank Barrera spoke along the same lines: "Do not give us a completed document conceived in absolute secrecy." He said bitterly, "We have been represented by the proponents as perpetual objectors to zoning resolutions in this city."[100]

The following day the hearing reconvened, and the pattern of opposition and advocacy developed more clearly. Many of the local business groups, especially in Queens, the Bronx, Brooklyn, and Staten Island, regarded the proposal with fear. The homeowners from the same areas favored the plan, often with excited enthusiasm, although many requested more restrictive bulk provisions for their areas.[101]

On March 18 the Planning Commission carried the debate to the boroughs, where the pattern of the city-wide hearings was repeated.[102] The city-wide, Reform-oriented associations all came forward to offer their support. There was evidence that the Planning Commission was gathering much of its grass-roots support from local homeowners' groups, but opposition was strong from local business and real estate associations.[103]

During the Staten Island hearing, on March 25, Felt revealed his effort to win Moses' support. He read a letter from Moses in which Moses said,

Staten Island is the only borough where the prompt adoption of a new zoning resolution or reasonable amendments within the framework of the new amendment can be really effective. The rest of the city is built up, and benefits which are finally derived from changes in the zoning resolution will appear slowly.[104]

This was at best a grudging concession, but it was a concession.

The March 25 hearing was the last of the series, and on April 8 the City Club summed up the results:

To political observers present at the recent hearings of the City Planning Commission, the news was how little strength the anti-zoning forces were able to muster. . . . Groups . . . had been largely won over by Chairman Felt's diplomatic handling of earlier objections and by well-balanced concessions.[105]

The Planning Commission was, perhaps, less certain. Granted that support had been encouragingly widespread, and granted also that the opposition showed signs of weakness, the battle was not won. The commission could now go to the Board of Estimate if it chose, for it had completed the mandatory formal hearings. But the commission announced that it would delay final submission of the plan until further revisions had been made and further hearings held. Felt apparently recognized that support was not general enough, that overwhelming grass-roots support and top echelon support from building and real estate interests had not yet come forth.

The staff began the task of collating the complaints that had come from the hearings and the painful task of bargaining the proposal to meet these complaints. This was not a happy labor.

As the summer wore on, some members of the staff and many of the Reform-oriented civic groups grew nervous at the extent of the concessions. Groups such as the Citizens Union, while publicly continuing their support, feared that any substance, any potential for change, was being lost in the effort to win unanimous support. Some of the Reformers felt that the commission should go to the Board of Estimate with the plan intact, before any victory became an empty shell:

Many of us felt that the whole thing was moving more and more towards the status quo. The intent was to have a new zoning resolution, one modeled for changing conditions. But the grace period was introduced, the nonconforming use provisions were disemboweled, the performance standards became meaningless, and a hundred or more incidental changes were introduced that made the whole code no more than a legalization of the existing state of things.

Nevertheless, these groups could not oppose the proposal; they could only work quietly in an effort to preserve its original "integrity." And while members of the planning staff might question the wisdom of the bargains struck, Felt had infused them with the desire to win, at any cost, if the Planning Commission was to have a meaningful role in the future development of the city.

The summer saw the hard bargains struck. A number of the city-wide business groups were given major parking concessions, the Fifth Avenue Association "practically drafted its own use district," the New York Real Estate Board was given milder bulk provisions, and the support of the homeowners was ensured with tighter bulk provisions for the outlying boroughs.

But on June 7, 1960, Moses delivered a scathing attack on the plan. He said the proposal was an "alphabet soup" and a "panacea." [106] Felt and Wagner moved to counter the attack, but they could not be sure of their success.[107] The Planning Commission could hope that it was now too late for the attack to affect the outcome. In a series of letters, however, Moses was gradually persuaded to take a more lenient view of the proposal.[108]

On June 28 the Planning Commission scheduled a final round of hearings for September, and it undertook the last rounds of bargaining and persuasion. On August 17 the Planning Commission released its last revision of the proposal.[109] To a large measure, the revisions ratified the agreements already made and anticipated possible future objections. Sections that were unpleasant to the Board of Standards and Appeals and the Parks Commissioner had been dropped. The parking requirements were relaxed. The nonconforming use requirements were profoundly altered, and a large number of mapping changes were included.

The final hearings had been scheduled for September 12, 13, and 14. On September 8 the Commerce and Industry Association and the Downtown–Lower Manhattan Association (a prestigious organization of realtor and financial organizations) offered their unqualified support.[110] On September 9 the New York Chapter of the AIA formally broke away from the Architects Council and endorsed the plan, carrying with it over half of the membership of the council.[111] On September 10 the New York Real Estate Board, without warning the other members of the Metropolitan Real Estate Boards Association, joined those favoring the proposal.[112]

Further, the only member of the Board of Estimate who had publicly opposed the proposal had been eliminated. Early in 1960, Hulan Jack had become embroiled in a scandal, the so-called Jack-Ungar scandal.[113] In April Jack had resigned from his office, thus removing this source of opposition.

On September 12, 1960, the hearings opened. It was clear that the Planning Commission had won the greatest part of its battle. Although the Brooklyn, Bronx, and Queens Real Estate Boards voiced their opposition, the Staten Island Real Estate Board–Chamber of Commerce coalition had joined the ranks of those supporting the revisions. The truncated Architects Council, under Max Simon's leadership, was still in opposition, as was the Queens Chamber of Commerce, but the rest of the hearings consisted of three days of almost monotonous repetition of support for the Planning Commission's revisions.

The last step was to the Board of Estimate. On October 18, 1960, the Planning Commission unanimously adopted the Comprehensive Amendment to the Zoning Resolution, as it had been revised on August 17.[114] The plan was forwarded to the Board of Estimate, which scheduled its hearings for November 21 and 22. Attention shifted to the members of the board. Last-minute efforts were made to reach the borough presidents by the opposing groups but

even though we knew that certain of the borough presidents did not like the proposals, they were no longer in a position to listen. Although certain members of the board opposed the resolution in principle and details, the Planning Commission had erected too impressive an appearance of widespread support. Besides, they had the mayor on their side, and he pressed the issue on every hand.

The Board of Estimate hearings had a large turnout—148 speakers appeared.[115] Of these, only nineteen spoke in opposition, the same groups that had opposed the proposal before the Planning Commission. Even the Building Industry League, which had long held out against the commission, spoke in favor of the proposal. On December 15, 1960, the Board of Estimate met to vote on the proposed resolution. The vote was unanimously in favor of the resolution, and it was passed without the board attempting to make changes in the plan.[116] After forty-four years, the city had a new comprehensive zoning resolution.

Victory: Substance or Symbol?

In the years 1949–53, the Planning Commission had three chairmen, offered a major proposal to rezone the city, and was defeated on that proposal. In 1956 James Felt was appointed chairman of the commision. The time was auspicious for another attempt at comprehensive rezoning. The "Reform Democrats" were gaining in power, Mayor Wagner was a strong political figure and sympathetic to city planning, and the city was physically changing at a rapid but not frenetic rate.

Felt undertook the fight for comprehensive rezoning. He threw huge resources into the struggle. The Planning Commission staff devoted thousands of man-hours to revising and propagandizing the Voorhees, Walker, Smith, and Smith plan. The Citizens Union, the City Club, the Regional Plan Association, and the Committee for Modern Zoning lobbied patiently and persistently for rezoning. Felt used his own contacts in the real estate and building worlds to persuade acquaintances and recruit supporters.

Those opposing the code were never able to coalesce into a unified front of opposition, and the Planning Commission worked consciously to increase the "natural" divisions in the opposition camp.

In December, 1960, the new Comprehensive Zoning Resolution was passed by unanimous vote of the Board of Estimate. A question still remained, however: Had the Planning Commission won a victory, or had it won only the satisfaction of seeing the Board of Estimate ratify the status quo? Was the new resolution a real innovation, true comprehensive rezoning, or was it merely the empty symbol of victory?

In fact, it may be decades before the question can be answered. The 1960 Zoning Resolution was a complex, apparently novel, and untested document. We can however, consider some of the factors that will have to be included in an answer to the question.

The Planning Commission could claim that the 1960 Resolution was, at least, different. Further, the new resolution limited the population of the city to slightly over twelve million as against the permitted fifty-five million under the 1916 Resolution. The performance standards were law; the nonconforming use provisions, for the first time in New York, were law.

On the other hand, the Planning Commission gave a major concession in the form of a grace period, which was finally prolonged into 1963 after two extensions were granted to the builders. The performance standards were considerably modified, and the nonconforming use provisions were bargained to the extent that they had very limited applicability.

The Planning Commission made roughly 1,000 amendments to the VWS&S plan. Of these, approximately 800 were offered in the December, 1959, revision. The greatest number of these were mapping changes. Stated on an areal basis, the concessions were made to win the support of the Manhattan-based architect, real estate, and business groups and to win the grass-roots support of homeowners in the other boroughs.

The fact is that the Planning Commission was forced to work within the context of goals which, if not in conflict, were at least not congruent. The doctrine of "comprehensive zoning" required that the Planning Commission search out the "general interest" of the city through rational, objective means. The demands of politics required the Planning Commission to seek support from those groups which were strategically placed, whose support was necessary to win votes on the Board of Estimate. This required the Planning Commission to bargain and make concessions that had no relation to the "comprehensiveness" of the rezoning plan.

In the final analysis, it appears that the political structure and processes of the city determined the extent of the Planning Commission's "victory." Considering the events of the 1930s and 1940s, the Planning Commission may have been pleased that it won anything at all.

PART TWO

PATTERNS
AND ANALYSIS

IV

THE GOVERNMENTAL
PARTICIPANTS
AND THE RULES
OF THE GAME

The preceding chapters have described the events in the history
of zoning in New York City. Although each major struggle over
zoning policy was unique in time, context, and outcome, it is
possible to look back over the events and to note certain
patterns. Some of these are fairly obvious: the role of the Reformers, the opposition of the borough presidents, the importance of the Board of Estimate, and the activities of interest
groups. Other patterns are more subtle: the divisions within
the interest group population, the differences between elected
leaders and administrative agencies, the patterns of interactions
among participants, and the special place of bargaining in the
zoning system.

The next three chapters will attempt to sort out and analyze
the most significant patterns in zoning in New York City.
Certain factors seem to persist over long periods of time and
to change only gradually. These "long-run" factors shaped the
actions of participants and resulted in consistencies of behavior
for the participants affected by them.[1] Among these are the
charter provisions, the written statutes, and the informal
expectations of participants that certain kinds of behavior were
permissible and other kinds were not. This congeries of formal

laws and informal expectations can be collectively called the "rules of the game."

There was another set of long-run determinants of behavior. All the participants had a definite stake or interest in particular zoning proposals and in zoning in general. We have seen, for example, that the borough presidents often viewed zoning as a threat to their "autonomy," or that realtors responded to zoning because of their interest in the city's land economy. These interests and stakes in zoning helped to form the way participants reacted to zoning proposals, and equally important, these interests changed only slowly (if at all) over a period of time.

Since the rules of the game and the actors' interests tended to determine the actions and the patterns of behavior and thereby the form that the zoning system took, we may say that these factors tend to give the zoning system a structure.

The Rules of the Game

The rules of the game occupied a special place in the structure of the zoning system. The formal rules were those provisions that were written into law (appearing in constitutions, charters, statutes, and administrative codes). The formal rules designated governmental agencies, offices, means of attaining these offices, the scope of authority of an agency, and the procedures and performances attached to office-holding or that were required of an agency.[2] The informal rules were less clear-cut but equally operative. They were the sets of expectations that were developed over a period of time and were accepted as binding by the participants.[3]

The rules of the game could be changed.[4] The Reformers of 1914 changed the formal rules when they sponsored legislation empowering the Board of Estimate to zone the city; and the Charter reform of 1938 changed the formal rules substantially.

But for any given struggle over a zoning proposal, the actors had to accept the rules as binding and had to accept the consequences imposed by the rules. Thus, the rules of the game helped to give a shape and form to the zoning system. As two observers of the general nature of politics in New York City have said, "The contest might deteriorate into a shapeless, even violent free-for-all if it were not for the existence and wide acceptance" of the rules.[5] Even further, the rules in zoning not only said what actors could or could not do, but they also said what governmental agencies were to be participants.

THE RULES: PRE–1938. Prior to 1938, the formal rules of the game gave three sets of governmental actors the major roles in zoning policy-making: the Board of Estimate, the Board of Standards and Appeals, and the borough building superintendents. The Board of Estimate had the greatest formal power: to initiate and to vote on all amendments or modifications of the Zoning Resolution.[6]

The Board of Estimate was not a unitary body, however. Composed of the mayor, the comptroller, the president of the Board of Aldermen, and the five borough presidents, it approximated a gathering of more or less powerful and autonomous chieftains.[7] The three city-wide officers had three votes apiece on the board, the borough presidents of Brooklyn and Manhattan two votes each, and the remaining boroughs one each (for a total of sixteen votes). It would seem that the city-wide officers had the power to control zoning on the Board of Estimate, since a majority vote was sufficient to amend the code. In fact, however, the operation of the informal rule of "borough courtesy" modified the formal situation. The tendency was to defer to the borough president whose jurisdiction was affected by the proposed change, in effect leading to a substantial modification of the distribution of votes on the board.[8] Accordingly, in vote after vote, any borough president whose borough was affected by the proposed change could count on the votes of all the other borough presidents and always on some or all of the city-wide members' votes.

Further, until 1938, the building superintendents worked directly out of the borough presidents' offices. These officials were formally charged with examining applications for building permits and comparing the applications with the provisions of the Zoning Resolution and the Building Code. Both codes were sufficiently flexible and vague to provide a wide degree of discretion for the individual superintendent.[9] If an applicant was dissatisfied with a decision by a building superintendent, or if the neighboring landowners were opposed to the decision, it could be appealed to the Board of Standards and Appeals, established for the purpose of hearing appeals.

The BSA was theoretically a "city-wide" body, representative of no particular borough, its members (or a majority of them) appointed by the mayor.[10] The powers of the BSA depended on the latitude provided in the Zoning Resolution. Under the 1916 Resolution it was charged with reviewing all cases of "unnecessary hardship." Although what constituted "unnecessary hardship" could be reviewed by the courts, the vagueness of the phrase provided the BSA a considerable range of discretion in setting its own rules and in handling cases coming to it. During the period 1916 to 1938, the BSA and the building superintendents were often engaged in jurisdictional disputes, each resenting the functions and discretionary powers of the other.[11]

In summary, the formal rules prior to the Charter reform of 1938 gave responsibility for the administration of the Zoning Resolution to three very different governmental actors. The informal rules tended to emphasize a "local" handling of zoning matters by placing generous powers in the hands of the borough presidents and the building superintendents. Each had wide degrees of discretion at both ends of the zoning process: the amendment of the code and the supervision of its application.

THE RULES: POST–1938. With the passage of the revised Charter in 1936, the formal administration of the Zoning Resolution was considerably readjusted. The Board of Estimate still had the final voice in approving or modifying amendments to the code, and the weighted voting system still stood.[12] With the introduction of the City Planning Commission, however, the formal procedures were radically modified.

All amendments to the resolution began in the Planning Commission, passed after a mandatory public hearing by a majority vote. The Board of Estimate could veto or amend a Planning Commission proposal only by a three-quarters majority.[13] The borough presidents as a bloc could not prevent an amendment to the Zoning Resolution nor, for that matter, could the city-wide officers. What appeared to be a powerful bias in favor of the Planning Commission had been built into the rules. The only exception to this bias was the "20 percent rule." This was the device relied upon by the Citizens Zoning Commission to defeat the Moses plan in 1945.

The borough president was shorn of some of his formal power by the 1938 Charter. Much of his jurisdiction over local improvements and developments was given to centralized city agencies; for one, the borough building superintendents were transferred to the city-wide Department of Buildings. The informal rule of borough courtesy still operated on the Board of Estimate, however, and the Charter of 1938 by no means eliminated the borough president as a factor in the zoning system.[14]

The Board of Standards and Appeals was untouched by the Charter Reformers of 1936—its formal power continued to depend on what the Zoning Resolution delegated to it. Its jurisdictional disputes were shifted to focus on the Department of Buildings and its new rival, the Planning Commission.

The Planning Commission was the major innovation in the formal structure of the zoning system. Composed of seven members, six appointed by the mayor for eight-year overlapping terms, it was provided with a staff of indefinite size, the director of which was also the chairman of the commission.[15] The Planning Commission was charged with the preparation of a master plan, a capital budget, and proposals to amend the Zoning Resolution as its three major functions. Thus, the Planning Commission became an intervening force in the older zoning system. Where zoning had formerly been handled by the borough presidents' offices and the building superintendents in the five separate boroughs, the Planning Commission represented both a new source of initiative and a centralization of the zoning process. Further, the Board of Standards and Appeals had operated under a Zoning Resolution that underwent only very minor modification. The Planning Commission theoretically could limit the BSA's jurisdiction and discretion over zoning questions through a revision of the Zoning Resolution (as was attempted in 1959, for example, with the proposal for a zoning administrator).

SUMMARY: THE FORMAL RULES. The Charter amendment of 1914 and the Zoning Resolution of 1916 gave the Board of Estimate, the borough building superintendents, and the Board of Standards and Appeals significant roles in the administration and amendment of the zoning code. "Borough courtesy" on the Board of Estimate acted to strengthen the informal authority of the borough presidents over zoning provisions.

In 1938, however, the formal rules of the game were considerably modified. The borough president's jurisdiction over local matters was reduced. The initiation and processing of zoning amendments was placed in the hands of the Planning Commission although the vote of the Board of Estimate was required for formal approval of changes. In general, the Charter of 1938 represented an effort to centralize control over the zoning system.

Governmental Actors and Interests

The rules of the game were a reflection of another structural factor in the zoning system: the stakes and interests that the actors brought to the system. The rules required certain actors to participate and, with participation, brought the interests of these actors into the system.

The *elected leaders* in the zoning system—that is, the members of the Board of Estimate—lived primarily in a world of electoral politics. Their survival—whether they remained in office for another term or not—depended on what happened on primary day and election day. To a large extent, they calculated their policy stands in terms of the effects that such stands might have on the party organization and on the electorate. Many of the elected leaders, of course, had real policy preferences and commitments. Mayor Walker fought long and hard for a planning commission, despite opposition from the party leaders. Both O'Dwyer and Wagner were committed to comprehensive zoning, and it is probable that without these commitments zoning policy-making would not have progressed as far as it did. La Guardia, on the other hand, had practically no concern with zoning whatsoever. The elected leaders nonetheless had to calculate their policy preferences in terms of the realities of party politics, and this often led to an inclination to remain neutral for as long as possible on zoning policy questions.

Each of the elected leaders, especially the mayor, the comptroller, and the borough presidents, also supervised a bureaucracy.[16] In addition to their concerns about party and electorate reactions, the elected leaders were forced also to calculate their policy stands in terms of the effects such policies might have on the administrative agencies over which they presided. The mayor's own effectiveness could be damaged by an overt conflict between the Planning Commission and the BSA, for example. The borough president had little desire to undercut the authority of the engineers serving in his office.

As a consequence, the elected leader approached commitments on zoning policy cautiously and, when making public decisions (as he must on the Board of Estimate), he attempted to relate his decision to his own preferences, and to the depth and breadth of opposition to or support for a zoning proposal: Were the nongovernmental groups members of his constituency? How far-reaching was support or opposition? What effect would a negative or favorable vote have on the leader's control of his segment of the city's bureaucracy? And, did he personally want or oppose the proposal so much that he was willing to accept the costs of ignoring the other factors?

The *administrative agencies* in the zoning system had a stake in zoning that was, like that of the elected leaders, related to survival and preference. These agencies, however, were not concerned with survival at the polls. Their major concern was with the survival of agency existence and function and pursuing a line of policy that conformed to the agency's goals and aspirations. The Board of Standards and Appeals, the Department of Buildings (after 1938), and the City Planning Commission lived in an environment in which they competed for allocations of funds, personnel, functions, and the good favor of the elected leaders. Often, also, these agencies were in conflict with each other in their particular construction of the role they felt they should play in the governmental system. The administrative agencies often strove to stabilize their respective environments by establishing routine patterns for solving problems and dealing with other governmental participants as well as their interest group constituencies.[17]

STAKES AND ACTORS: PRE-1938. The Reformers of 1913–16

created a Zoning Resolution for New York City. To do so, they felt impelled not only to listen to the demands of interest groups but to bring the Board of Estimate and the Board of Standards and Appeals into the zoning process. The change in the formal rules that empowered the Board of Estimate to zone the city introduced the members of the board and their interests into zoning.

The members of the Board of Estimate were closely linked to the *party organizations,* especially during the 1920s and 1930s. But the party organizations were likely to be only peripherally interested in the substantive context of zoning as public policy. The party leaders were not anxious to advocate specific bulk or use restrictions; at best such stands could only alienate some segments of the electorate. The party leaders were, however, brokers for claims made against the Zoning Resolution. They could expedite these claims to the appropriate agencies and reap the benefits of a favor done for a friend. A Manhattan real estate lawyer and party official during the 1920s and 1930s expressed his concern for zoning:

During the 1920s and 1930s I was not concerned with whether the zoning said this area was to be industrial or that area residential. . . . As a local party officer I might have occasion to help someone in difficulty with the zoning law or with the Board of Standards and Appeals. But this was routine work, a result of my knowledge about city government and affairs that would allow me to assist a local citizen and voter in the conduct of his affairs.

The county leaders and the lesser district leaders were the centers of power for the party organizations in New York City.[18] These party officials were primarily concerned with the complexities of winning office and controlling the party organization. If helping a friend of the party would aid them in these tasks, then these leaders had a stake in zoning, but it was not a stake that was tied directly to the policy content of zoning.

The struggle over Mayor Walker's proposal to establish a

planning department demonstrated an important point, however. The party leaders were committed to the local administration of the zoning code. The Brooklyn and Bronx Democratic
organizations joined Tammany Hall in fighting the proposal
in 1929, and it was not until the borough organizations decided
that Walker's final proposal was not a threat that they
relented in their opposition.[19]

The *borough presidents,* as elected members of the Board of
Estimate and sharing the same electoral base as the party
county leaders, had a similar stake in zoning. The interest of
the borough presidents was, however, more extensive and more
immediate than that of the party organizations. Their routine
activities were concerned with borough administration. They
daily worked with local interest groups, and the local groups
turned to them for help in zoning problems. The close tie of
the borough president, as elected leader and as borough administrative officer, to the local party organizations only reinforced this bond. Borough autonomy dictated that the borough
president be responsible for handling local matters, and borough courtesy on the Board of Estimate was an informal
recognition of the stake the borough president had in the
symbiotic relation among interest group demands, party needs,
and administrative claims.

Zoning proposals were processed through the borough presidents' offices. Initially zoning changes were the concern of the
borough building superintendents, who were directly subordinate to the borough president and the borough engineer.[20]
The transfer of this function to a city-wide department meant
that the borough president was deprived of a source of control
over local affairs and that the functions of his staff were under
attack. Understandably, the borough presidents fought Walker's plan for a City Planning Board in 1929 and 1930, and they
fought the Charter reformers' proposal for a City Planning
Commission in 1934–36. These battles were attempts to

preserve not only the structure of party politics as the city then knew it but also the borough president's control over his jurisdiction.

The *mayor, the comptroller,* and *the president of the Board of Aldermen* were the three most prominent elected leaders on the Board of Estimate. Of these, the mayor was by far the most conspicuous. These three officials rarely showed any real interest in zoning. In spite of the seemingly dominant position the city-wide elected leaders held on the Board of Estimate, the localism inherent in the party system and the zoning system of the pre-1938 period dampened their interest in zoning. Hylan and Walker, particularly, seemed more than willing to leave the administration and amendment of the Zoning Resolution to the borough presidents and their allies.

The major exception in the pattern of behavior of the elected leaders was, of course, the *Fusion-elected leaders.* McAneny, as borough president of Manhattan and later president of the Board of Aldermen, and Mitchel as mayor had their electoral base in the Fusion movement of 1910–16. Aside from the support that they depended upon—the support of the Citizens Union, the City Club, and other Reform-oriented organizations and voters—their personal commitments and policy preferences led them to be strong proponents and active advocates of comprehensive zoning.

La Guardia, elected in 1933 as a Fusion mayor, had little interest in city planning and zoning, but he endorsed the idea of a City Planning Commission in response to his constituency and because he believed that the Planning Commission would weaken the power of the borough "machines." [21]

It should be noted, however, that the Fusion borough presidents were less amenable to comprehensive zoning and the idea of a city-wide planning agency than the mayor. Although Palma, Staten Island borough president in 1936, and Queens Borough President Harvey both ran as "Fusionists," they opposed establishing a City Planning Commission and favored keeping zoning in local hands.[22]

In the years before the Charter reform of 1936, the *Board of Standards and Appeals* was the major administrative agency concerned with the Zoning Resolution. The BSA was closely tied to the party organizations. Although the mayor made the majority of appointments to the BSA, apparently he was expected to clear these appointments with the borough organizations.[23] The BSA's attitude toward the administration of the zoning code was thus inevitably locally oriented.

The BSA was also strongly influenced by its interest group constituency. By law, the membership of the BSA was composed of architects, engineers, and building contractors.[24] Often these members of the BSA had no particular qualifications other than their party loyalty and the fact that they were satisfactory to the professional groups from which they were drawn. The real estate organizations, architects' groups, and building associations were adamant in sharing a voice with the party organizations in making appointments to the BSA.[25]

The stake of the BSA in zoning was not limited to the demands of party leaders and interest groups, however. Since the BSA's discretion over zoning questions depended on the provisions of the Zoning Resolution, the agency took a strongly defensive attitude toward the code. It scrutinized proposed changes carefully for any sign that an amendment might lessen its jurisdiction and constantly advocated changes that would broaden its role and discretion.[26]

The Board of Standards and Appeals had, as a consequence, a threefold stake in zoning. Its party ties, its interest group constituency, and its own commitments as an administrative agency gave it strong links to the content and processes of zoning administration.

The *borough building superintendents* were also closely linked to the administration of zoning. As appointees of the borough president, and as the officials who first examined building applications for conformity to the Zoning Resolution, the superintendents were committed to protecting their administrative discretion and preserving the control of the borough president by continuing local administration of the resolution. They were required to satisfy the borough president's constituents and to defend their own prerogatives against the occasional incursions of the BSA.

The pattern of formal and informal rules and the interests of the governmental actors prior to 1938 was that of a strong tendency toward local control of zoning questions. The elected leaders' stake in zoning was related to their party interests and their concern over their particular bureaucracies—although personal policy preferences occasionally led to deviations from this pattern. With the exception of the Fusion-elected leaders, the city-wide officers allowed administration of the Zoning Resolution to gravitate to the borough presidents, who fiercely defended their prerogatives. The administrative agencies—the Board of Standards and Appeals and the building superintendents—were also subject to the influence of the party organizations, the borough presidents, and the local interest groups.

GOVERNMENT ACTORS AND INTERESTS: POST–1938. The system of rules, actors, and interests established by the Reformers of 1913–16 persisted with little change until 1938. The resistance of the borough presidents and the borough party leaders to the proposals for a city-wide planning agency during 1929 and 1934–36 was testimony to the workability of the system. The indifference of so many interest groups to the proposed Planning Commission in the Charter revision of 1936 also bore witness to the proposition that the pre-1938 zoning system was rooted basically in the party-system–rules-of-the-game complex.

Significantly, the structure of the pre-1938 zoning system was based on the inherent localism of New York City party and borough politics. La Guardia and Reform-Fusion came to power in 1933 dedicated to opposing the borough "machines" and the localism that they represented. The Reformers were determined to centralize the city government's structure, and the Charter of 1938 was the product of their efforts.

During the years of the La Guardia administration and after, moreover, the role of the *party organization* underwent a major change. In 1936 La Guardia and Fusion had already held City Hall and many of the borough presidencies for three years. Widespread and flagrant distribution of patronage was no longer part of the rules of the party game. Patronage was still distributed in the years from 1933 to 1960, but in a more discreet fashion and with more attention to the skills required in the job to which the appointment was being made.[27]

La Guardia weakened the regular party organizations. The years following 1945 continued this trend. Although the Brooklyn and Bronx organizations continued to be major forces in the party politics of the city, Tammany Hall slipped badly. Population shifts, poor leadership, and the rise of the Reform Democrats all weakened the Manhattan Democratic organization.[28] During the 1950s Carmine De Sapio attempted to give Tammany a "new image," but with only short-lived success. Wagner followed La Guardia's method: he attacked the "bosses" to win the support of the Reformers, and he dealt with the Regulars when he felt it was necessary.

The consequence of the diminishing role of the old-line party organizations was a decrease of interest in zoning for the borough organizations. The advent of the Planning Commission, the enhanced role of the city-wide officers on the Board of Estimate, and the decreased authority of the borough presidents limited the function of the party leaders as funnels for claims against the Zoning Resolution. Thus it was possible for one participant to say:

Zoning is really nonpartisan. Both sides—those opposed to a particular proposal or those in favor of it—try to gather as many supporters as possible, and they will try to include party leaders if they can be persuaded to commit themselves. But the party leaders have no interest in it, they have nothing to gain. No one goes to a district leader to get the zoning law changed anymore, and if they did, it would do no good. The party leaders have too many other things to worry about than zoning.

The diminished stake of the party organizations in zoning was partly a result of the changed role of the *borough presidents* in the zoning system. The Charter of 1938 had been intended to reduce the power of the borough president not only on the Board of Estimate but also within his own jurisdiction in the borough. The effort was partly successful. The 1938 Charter stripped the borough president of many of his routine but important local functions. No longer did zoning proposals formally originate in the borough president's office to be cleared by the party organization and carried to the Board of Estimate where borough courtesy would determine the outcome. And no longer was the building superintendent under his complete and immediate supervision. The old bonds between interest group, party organization, and Borough Hall in zoning matters were destroyed by the Charter of 1938.

The stake of the borough president in zoning continued, however. The functions that the 1938 Charter left to the borough president—care and maintenance of borough streets, routine engineering and public works projects, and other physical services—still gave the borough president wide and frequent contact with local building associations, homeowners, and real estate organizations. Further, the borough president still had an interest in preserving borough autonomy, an interest that was perhaps heightened as autonomy was reduced. Lyons consistently opposed major zoning proposals from 1939 to 1960, and he opposed them because he saw the Planning Commission as a threat to his traditional prerogatives as borough president of the Bronx. Although the borough president had "the formal capacity to claim that he speaks, as no other member of the Board of Estimate can, for the special interests of his borough," [29] the Planning Commission represented a constant threat to go over his head to the local interest groups in his borough. And, in the years after 1938, interest groups did, in fact, go increasingly often to the Planning Commission or the mayor in their efforts to promote or block zoning proposals. The borough president was thus forced more and more to take a negative attitude toward zoning. Each proposal was an implicit, if not explicit, attack on his ability to satisfy the needs of his constituency. His negative votes on the Board of Estimate in 1940 and 1944 were expressions of this defensive attitude.

The borough president, in the years following 1938, had a decreased party interest in zoning, but his stake in zoning was not eliminated by the Charter of 1938. He was still forced to fight for the survival of his office, his functions, and the pattern of relations that he built up with his interest group constituency.

The role of the *mayor* had changed also. No longer did he appear as "belonging" to the borough organizations. La Guardia set a precedent for strong leadership, and the added formal powers of the mayoralty in the new Charter made it an even more conspicuous office. The mayor became one of the principal targets of groups advocating or opposing zoning proposals. Further, he appointed the members of the Planning Commission, and this gave at least O'Dwyer and Wagner a sense of commitment to the programs of that agency. Although La Guardia and Impellitteri showed little interest in the Planning Commission or zoning, La Guardia, with sufficient prompting from the Reform-oriented groups, supported rezoning in 1940 and 1944. But the mayor's stake in zoning was still influenced by how he computed electoral risks and the probabilities of controlling his giant bureaucracy. As one city planner who was in a position to know said:

In 1960, Wagner had to ask himself: What does my support mean? If I push on zoning will the borough presidents or the comptroller or the Buildings department torpedo other programs? He had to ask himself what enemies he might make, and what friends. He had to ask whether this was the best time, or would some other time produce more effective results. The decision was probably not an easy one.

If the mayor were to be the active proponent of a popular and successful zoning proposal, he stood to benefit from the favorable reactions of the civic associations, the Planning Commission, and possibly other groups benefiting from the plan.[30] An ill-conceived or premature support of an unpopular plan could be a liability, however. The mayor's support was necessary for the passage of a comprehensive zoning proposal, but this endorsement was usually offered slowly. The mayor had to be convinced that general support of the plan existed before he would give his support.[31]

The other city-wide officers on the Board of Estimate, the *comptroller* and the *president of the Council,* occupied a position similar to that of the mayor, with the added advantage (or disadvantage) of being less conspicuous. These two officers seem to have taken their cues from the mayor on zoning issues. All three had a common constituency, and it appears that the comptroller and the president of the Council felt that, if the risk were a reasonable one for the mayor, it was for them also.

The *City Planning Commission* was the major innovation in the formal rules of the zoning system in the 1938 Charter. The Planning Commission represented the formal installation of the Reformer's "city-wide" and "general" view of the public interest in the structure of the government. It was protected from "political" (that is, party) influence through the provisions that made it difficult for any one mayor to appoint a majority of the Planning Commission members and that made an extraordinary majority on the Board of Estimate necessary to block commission proposals. The commission's functions also represented both a major innovation and the Reformers' biases. Master planning, capital budgeting, and the initiation of zoning proposals were to be the three instruments for controlling the physical development of the city. That these duties were given to the City Planning Commission meant that the Charter reformers hoped not only that these functions would be "above politics" but that they would be approached from a comprehensive perspective.

The Planning Commission was thus an administrative agency whose major duties were coordination and innovation. And these functions were a constant irritant to other governmental agencies. The commission was in existence for less than a year before it was charged with "raiding" the functions and personnel of other agencies.[32] Its initial requests for personnel were temporarily blocked, and then for ten years it had no further staff increases.[33]

Its first effort at master planning was unsuccessful, and capital budgeting rapidly became a meaningless function. As a consequence, the stake of the Planning Commission in comprehensive zoning increased in direct proportion to its failures in its other areas. By 1953 the morale of the commission was low, it could not fill the staff vacancies it had, and many staff members were leaving for positions that paid as much as twice the salary the commission could offer.[34] The only way the Planning Commission could correct the situation, as it saw the matter, was through a concrete achievement in comprehensive zoning. Felt came to the Planning Commission determined to win this achievement and to win a friendly constituency. The interest of the Planning Commission in zoning began as the stake of the Reformer in a "general" approach to urban problems. It soon became a struggle for the existence of the agency and the existence of the agency's functions. The failures of the zoning attempts in 1940, 1945, and 1953 only served to increase the commitment of the Planning Commission to comprehensive zoning.

The *Board of Standards and Appeals,* although formally unchanged by the Charter of 1938, was no longer the creature of the party organizations by the time the Charter went into effect. In 1932 Harris Murdock was appointed chairman of the BSA. Murdock, an engineer with a precise and austere mind, "cleaned up" the BSA.[35] He insisted on a literal interpretation of the Zoning Resolution and broke the old ties with the party organizations. In exchange for the links with the county party organizations, the BSA created a comfortable working relation with the builders, architects, and realtors that appeared before it. Although the interest groups occasionally chafed under Murdock's meticulous interpretation of the Zoning Resolution, they were quick to oppose any effort to curtail the BSA's powers.[36]

Although the BSA was no longer tied to the Zoning Resolution through the party organizations, its stake in zoning remained high. The BSA still depended on the provisions of the resolution for its jurisdiction over zoning. The Planning Commission's occasional proposals to reduce the BSA's discretionary powers were treated by Murdock as direct threats to the existence and functions of his agency.

The *Department of Buildings* and the Planning Commission were the BSA's two chief rivals, even though the Department of Buildings existed in a situation similar to the BSA. The department was also dependent on the provisions of the Zoning Resolution for its discretion in zoning, and it could view the efforts of the Planning Commission only as attempts to limit its authority. The department's interest group relations were never entirely amicable,[37] and this apparently only sharpened its anxiety at the Planning Commission's innovative efforts.

One participant described the place of the BSA and the Department of Buildings in these terms:

The Board of Standards and Appeals has to be understood for what it is. In some ways it has never recovered from the Seabury Investigations [of the early 1930s] that portrayed it as a center of graft and corruption. The board is very nervous about attempts to limit its authority or suggestions that it might be behaving improperly. I think the board has been a captive of the pressure groups who appeal to it. It serves as a refuge for those who want to avoid the Zoning Resolution, but this is not the whole explanation.

The Department of Housing and Buildings is in a similar position. Both the department and the Board of Standards and Appeals are frequently targets of corruption and inefficiency. There may be enough truth in both accusations to make them shy of reforming proposals. Both the board and the Buildings people are sensitive to efforts to reduce their authority, but in New York who isn't? In addition both departments play an important role in the implementation and enforcement of zoning. The Planning Commission must take their attitudes into account. If they are entirely displeased with a zoning amendment they can either enforce it only halfheartedly or else appeal to the mayor, who will certainly at least listen to them. No mayor wants unnecessary strife in his departments, so often he will encourage an attitude on the part of the planners to avoid strife.

The *courts* occupied a special position in the zoning system throughout the period 1910 to 1960.[38] These governmental agencies rarely became involved in the problems and conflicts around comprehensive zoning, although they acted as a place of resort for participants who were dissatisfied with the existing Zoning Resolution. As evidenced by Bassett's search for a legal, constitutional ground on which to formulate comprehensive zoning and the effectiveness of the CZC in overturning the Moses plan, the courts stood as a brooding threat to proposals that were too innovative or too far out of line with the existing functioning of the political system.

Ordinarily, the authority of the courts was felt in the routine administration of the zoning code, where their decisions on appeals made from the Board of Standards and Appeals could strongly influence particular local struggles and the rule-making power of the BSA.

Over the fifty-year period, the local and state courts tended to take an increasingly permissive attitude toward innovations in zoning practices, although they frequently construed narrowly the power of the building superintendents and the BSA to vary the code. Under Murdock, the BSA had relatively fewer collisions with the courts than under his predecessors, probably because Murdock himself was inclined toward a strict interpretation of the Zoning Resolution.

Other governmental agencies appeared as more or less frequent participants in the zoning process. The Department of Parks, the Department of Traffic, and the Port of New York Authority had specialized (although often peripheral) interests in zoning proposals affecting their jurisdictions.[39] These agencies apparently felt that they should be consulted before zoning proposals were offered that might touch on parking provisions, the location (or environment) of parks, and similar problems. In general, however, these agencies showed only a limited concern with comprehensive zoning.

Resources

Of all the governmental participants in the zoning system, the elected leaders would appear to have had the greatest resources for asserting their claims and protecting their interests. The formal rules provided them with votes on the Board of Estimate—votes with which they could bargain if not defeat (or enact) a proposal. In addition, they possessed a link with the party organizations, a resource that varied depending on the party in power at a particular point in time or with the viability of the organization, but nonetheless an asset.

The Fusion mayors suffered from the disadvantage that their "organizations" were usually loosely structured and often amorphous coalitions and that Reform-Fusion usually had a short life-span. The Regular mayors tended to suffer from the other extreme: they were too often dependent on the party organization, and the price of independent action might be defeat on primary or election day.

Party as a resource in zoning politics declined. The borough presidents, who depended on party the most in the pre-La Guardia days, found themselves increasingly fighting a defensive battle. In the place of party as a resource, access to the mass media, to the bureaucracy, and to the broad-based interest groups became more significant. In this shift, the borough president suffered; the city-wide officers, especially the mayor, gained.

The borough president, both before and after the Charter of 1938, counted his close tie to the local interest groups and his role as spokesman for borough interests as his major political resource. To the extent these factors were realities, the borough president had a backing of considerable force, and even more so when borough courtesy was operative. Charter reform undermined many of the bases for this backing—the City Planning Commission was able to go to "the grass roots" and to speak through its public hearings and occasionally through the mayor as representative of not only local interests but, in the words of its own pet slogan, "the general interest."

The greatest resource of the Planning Commission, and one only occasionally used, was its staff. In general, relations between the commission chairman and the staff were congenial and cooperative and, when Felt utilized the staff to its fullest capacity, it was a potent implement for undermining opposition and generating support. The liabilities of the Planning Commission centered around its inability to create any permanent interest group constituency and the fact that it chronically had to confront hostile borough presidents on the Board of Estimate.

The Board of Standards and Appeals and the Department of Buildings had the resources of membership in the city bureaucracy and (to the extent that it existed) support from outside interest groups. Both could be an advantage in providing them with the leverage to bargain with other participants in the system, but both could be sources of conflict and instability as well.

Summary

The rules of the game and the interests of the governmental participants helped to determine the structure of the zoning system. In the years before the Charter of 1938, the rules and interests of the actors emphasized a local, borough-oriented administration of zoning policy. Although the political party organizations followed a "neutral" policy, they had an interest in preserving the localism of zoning. This localism was further reflected in the borough presidents, the Board of Standards and Appeals, and the building superintendents.

The Charter of 1938 modified the formal structure of the zoning system, however. The borough presidents were shorn of some of their formal authority, and the Planning Commission was introduced to administer zoning from a "general and comprehensive" viewpoint. Further, changes in the nature of party politics in the city reduced the interest of the borough party organizations in zoning.

The change in the rules of the game and in the interests of the participants was toward a centralization of the zoning process. The borough presidents and the BSA, however, retained their stake in zoning and opposed the encroachments of the Planning Commission. The mayor increased in prominence and his stake in zoning was enhanced. Nevertheless, the mayor and the other elected leaders still gauged their stands on zoning in terms of the risks involved.

V

THE NONGOVERNMENTAL PARTICIPANTS

Zoning affects a broad array of interests—economic, social, and ideological—in addition to the stakes of the governmental actors. As important as the governmental actors are, they must share the stage with the organized interest groups who attempt to influence zoning policy-making.

The Nongovernmental Actors

Characteristically, the nongovernmental participants in the zoning system are organized groups. Individuals, such as Bassett, Latham Squire, and Robert Dowling, to name a few, have played an important role in shaping zoning policy. In general, however, these individuals have acted as leaders; their major resource has been the organizational backing they brought to struggles over zoning. And a group leader must to some extent conform to the pressures of the organization that he is leading.[1]

While a group is a bringing-together of individuals who may share common interests and goals, there are limitations on the commonalty of even shared interests. The pressure of overlapping memberships, of differences of opinions among group members, and the tendencies toward fractionation in New York City created problems for many of the major interest group leaders. In 1960, for example, James Felt could appeal to the individual members of the real estate boards for support and thus undermine opposition from group leaders.

The organized interest groups nonetheless played a significant role in zoning. A major characteristic of these nongovernmental actors was their localism. Their stakes in zoning were most often rooted in specific geographic areas, occasionally defined as the entire borough, although more often (in numerical terms) confined to narrower areas. There were important exceptions—the broad-based business associations and civic associations, for example—but often even these groups were limited in the scope of their concern with zoning.

The Economic Interests

The nongovernmental groups in the zoning system brought their particular stakes to the contest. Each group tended to show a central tendency of interest, leading it to align itself in a specific way and to focus its interest on fairly specific aspects of zoning. Since zoning has strong economic overtones, affecting the land market, the location of business and industrial enterprises, and the economic growth of the city, it is not surprising that a large number of groups concentrated on the economic aspects of zoning.

THE BUILDING GROUPS.[2] The "building industry" was a far from homogeneous or monolithic grouping. It included organizations of builders, contractors, material suppliers, and certain labor groups.

These groups generally had less interest in zoning than in other building regulations of the city government. The Building Code and the Multiple Dwelling Code, for example, specified the materials, practices, and workmanship in a detailed fashion and thus affected the activities of the building industry in a far more direct fashion than the more generalized provisions of the Zoning Resolution. The principal building organizations, however, recognized that zoning could limit population density and growth and thereby also limit future building activity.

B. G. Levine (for the Kings County Homebuilders Association): Bulk cuts lead to adverse effects—to a stoppage in building activity, which leads to a loss in population and revenue, leading to blight and ruin.[3]

The threat was indirect, but it was a real one, as the building industry groups saw the matter. In general, the building industry groups translated their fears into opposition to bulk reductions, that is, reduction of the size of buildings. They tended to ignore the other provisions of particular zoning proposals:

Mr. Lindenbaum (of the Associated Builders of New York): The important thing is the bulk that our organization is concerned with.
Chairman Felt (of the Planning Commission): What about non-conforming uses?
Mr. Lindenbaum: Our organization of builders is not concerned with non-conforming uses.[4]

The building organizations that represented the outlying boroughs—the Associated Builders of New York (whose membership was largely drawn from Queens and Brooklyn) and the Staten Island Home Builders Association, for example—were more sensitive to restrictive bulk provisions than the Manhattan-based groups. This borough-oriented difference stemmed from the more fluid state of building activity in Queens, Staten Island, and Brooklyn particularly and from the fact that bulk provisions for these boroughs were often more restrictive than for the more intensively developed areas.[5]

The labor unions engaged in building activities shared the views of the other building industry groups. They objected to bulk provisions that would perhaps reduce construction of new buildings and thus reduce the number of jobs available to union membership. In 1914, the Union of Building Trades Employees of Manhattan and Brooklyn opposed the work of the Second Zoning Commission because limitation of building heights would lead to unemployment; [6] in 1944 and 1945, other labor organizations took similar stands toward the Moses plan.[7]

The stake of the labor organizations in zoning, however, seems to be even less clearly perceived than that of the other building associations. The labor unions tended to have more direct and pressing problems than changes in zoning.[8]

THE ARCHITECTS' GROUPS.[9] The interest groups representing the architectural profession showed more concern over the specifics of zoning than did the builders' groups. This concern stemmed in some measure from the architects' ideological commitment to city planning, but it also came from the economic stake that the architects had in zoning policy.

Traditionally the architect was the caretaker, practitioner, and voice of city planning. He took a proprietary and professional interest in planning based on the long influence that architecture had in planning and the architect's competence to handle the vocabulary and subject matter of zoning. [10] The architects' groups often took a role as "objective" critics of the City Planning Commission on zoning questions. Aside from this olympian view, there is a further dimension to the architects' interest. The architect must pursue his profession within the confines of the Zoning Resolution, and his task was made easier and more economical—or less so—depending on the provisions of the code in force. And, like the building groups, the architect has been sensitive to proposals that might lead to a reduction of building and hence his professional practice.

The major architectural groups were the five borough chapters of the American Institute of Architects.[11] The oldest and largest of these was the New York (Manhattan) Chapter, which claimed as members nine hundred of the seventeen hundred practicing architects in the city in 1960. These groups were the recognized "official" organizations for the architectural profession, and few if any practicing architects were not members.

In 1951 the five borough architectural groups joined forces

in the Architects Council, which had representatives from each of the borough organizations and was intended to speak with a single voice for the entire profession on all matters of common concern, including zoning. On zoning matters, however, the council had at least one restive member in the New York Chapter of the AIA, and so the council tended to represent the organizations of the outlying boroughs.

The principal line of division on zoning occurred between the "big" and "little" architectural firms and their representative organizations. In effect, this was a split between the New York Chapter and the other borough organizations. The New York Chapter, besides being the largest organization in membership, included on its rosters the majority of the larger individual firms. The division arose out of the difference of interest and stake in zoning policy. The larger firms had greater capability to deal with changing regulations. Also, since many of the larger firms practiced outside the city as well as within, their commitment to local building activity was less high than for the more localized firms. As one architect said:

When you have learned to work with one zoning resolution, learned one Bible so to speak, it is very difficult to convert to another. This is especially true of the smaller firm. There are costs involved in working under a new code, costs in time, in money, in litigation, and often in appeals. These costs damage the smaller firm more than the larger.

Many of the smaller firms derived a considerable part of their business from "conversions"—that is, cutting larger residential units into smaller ones—and this activity could be severely handicapped by lowered bulk provisions and less permissive variance procedures. Conversions were anathema to the City Planning Commissioners and conflict resulted between the goals of the City Planning Commission and the stakes of the Brooklyn, Queens, and Staten Island architects, especially. But the New York (Manhattan) Chapter of the AIA, with a membership designing large-scale building projects, was concerned chiefly with a resolution that provided a "flexible envelope," a code which was permissive toward large developments and also allowed a greater chance for design freedom.

While all the architectural groups showed a common concern over the question of bulk, the division among the borough organizations in their specific concerns resulted in a division among them on the content of the zoning proposals: the New York (Manhattan) Chapter of the AIA was frequently at odds with other organizations.

THE REAL ESTATE GROUPS.[12] Of all the nongovernmental actors, the realtors felt themselves to be most immediately affected by the economic consequences of zoning. Individuals and firms directly involved in land sales, management, and development from 1910 to 1960 were consistently in close attendance on zoning as public policy. The realtors eyed zoning from the viewpoint of those who were vulnerable to shifts in policy that might affect the fluctuations of the urban land market.

Although all realtors had a common general stake in the land values of the city, there were differences within the real estate profession. As one realtor perhaps overstated the fact, "There are as many different interests and viewpoints in the real estate 'community' as there are separate pieces of property and the purposes of owning it."

One of the major divisions in the real estate "community" occurred between the owners and managers on one hand and the developers on the other.[13] The real estate owners lived in an economic situation where the protection of a specific investment or set of investments was more critical than the promotion of future expansion. Their stake in zoning was largely one of defending (and perhaps enhancing) the conditions that led them to make the original investment. As a result, the owners paid more attention to those provisions of zoning proposals that touched on the existing state of things—most particularly the provisions governing nonconforming uses.

The developers, however, were committed to deriving the maximum future benefit from their investments by establishing an environment in which land values were constantly increasing. They were inextricably bound to an expanding real estate market, and were the first to feel the pinch that might come in a retardation of values. The developers were most seriously hurt by the decline of real estate values in the period prior to the Resolution of 1916, for example. The developer naturally turned his attention to zoning proposals that might cause increased development costs, that might reduce rentable or salable area, and that might halt expansion of the urban land market. Consistently the bulk provisions in zoning proposals were the major threats to the developers' interests, as they tended to reduce the size of buildings and thus increase costs while decreasing future rents and profits.

The organized interest groups of the real estate "community" were led by the five borough real estate boards, although there were other groups, such as the New York Taxpayers Association (principally owner oriented), the Jamaica (Queens) Real Estate Board, and other sub-borough organizations.

The borough real estate boards were represented in a "peak" association, the Metropolitan Real Estate Boards Association, which was founded in 1937, and which was composed of the presidents and executive secretaries of each of the borough boards (plus the Westchester County Real Estate Board). The chairmanship of the MREBA was rotated annually among the presidents of its constituent borough members. It had no staff or permanent headquarters as such. Its fundamental purpose was to bring the real estate boards together for discussion of matters of common concern and to propose and undertake "political action." Although the MREBA issued policy statements nominally for all of the five members from the city, in reality the borough organizations had nearly complete autonomy.

The New York Real Estate Board (Manhattan) was the oldest and the largest of the five boards. Founded in 1896 as a "getting together of the real estate brokers for mutual protection and benefits," [14] it was formally incorporated in 1912 and the following year expanded its membership base to include not only brokers but owners and anyone else "interested" in real estate matters. It undertook an independent line of action, breaking away from the then peak association—the Advisory Council of Real Estate Interests—in 1916. At the same time, the New York Board adopted a policy of expansion. By absorbing the Realty League in 1913 and aggressively seeking membership, it increased its rosters from 550 members in 1913 to 1,700 members by 1927 and to over 3,000 by 1960.[15] The New York Real Estate Board had a diversified membership by the 1920s, including not only brokers and owners but a number of building firms and almost the entire list of the major financial institutions of the city (who were themselves often real estate owners).

The other real estate boards were lesser scale models of the New York Board. Their memberships neither were as broadly based nor had the same degree of prestige as the Manhattan based organization.

Not surprisingly the "big-little" split evidenced in the architectural profession and expressed in borough terms appeared also in the real estate organizations. While harmony never characterized the real estate groups on zoning questions, the tension between the larger and smaller firms and the organizations that represented each of them was persistent over a period of time.[16]

While this division was not expressed solely as a division

among the boroughs, this was one of its principal manifesta-
tions. The smaller firms who were constituent members of the
boards in the "outlying" boroughs felt that zoning operated
against their interests and in favor of Manhattan, especially in
terms of bulk provisions. In the words of one realtor from an
outlying borough:

It has steadily been the policy of the City Planning Commission
to make it easier to assemble large projects and to make the smaller
plots of land more uneconomical to use. In general, this has had
the effect of favoring the big Manhattan developers who have
readier access to financing and can handle the long-term, costly
type of operation involved. In specific terms, the very provisions of
the zoning proposals (in 1949 and 1959) were specifically more
favorable to Manhattan in bulk provisions than for the other
boroughs. Out here I have had realtors come to me and say since
1960, "What'll I do now? They have taken my practice away from
me. I can't find anyone interested in any kind of project."

An outgrowth of the division of interests among the boards
was that the New York Board was usually the last to oppose
and the first to favor a new zoning proposal. On at least one
occasion, moreover (in 1960), the New York Board broke with
the Metropolitan Real Estate Boards Association without
consulting the other members of the association. The New
York Board, however, and the other real estate organizations
all showed a common tenderness in the area of nonconforming
uses. The nonconforming use proposals were a constant threat—
and not only to existing structures. Since the possibility of an
extension of the nonconforming use principle (once accepted)
might introduce an unstable factor into realty values and expectations, these provisions could make the gathering of
financial backing for real estate investments difficult if not
impossible.

The realtor also faced another disturbing problem. In the
zoning morality play he felt that he occupied the role of the
villain—the "antiprogressive," the landlord (or worse, the

"slumlord"), the rent-gouger, and the exploiter of the general interest to favor his own special interests.[17] As one observer of real estate practice and procedure put it:

The realtor is as necessary to developing the growth of the city as anyone, and perhaps more so since he takes the economic risks; at the same time he is usually painted as a moneygrubber. This is inclined to make him pretty sensitive, pretty quick to feel that every new zoning change is aimed directly at him. And, frequently, let's face it, it is.

THE CITY-WIDE BUSINESS GROUPS.[18] The groups whose memberships represented the major business, industrial, and financial firms had geographic bases including the entire city (and beyond) and accordingly diversified interests; they nonetheless showed a strong interest in zoning. The best known of these groups were the New York Chamber of Commerce, the Citizens Budget Commission, and the Commerce and Industry Association (earlier known as the Merchants Association). These groups saw themeslves as having a stake in zoning, although this was usually represented in a highly general fashion. They carried the authority of being the spokesmen for "big business," and these groups' involvements were multifold, carrying them not only to City Hall but to Albany and Washington. All were well and permanently staffed and all had impressive membership rosters.

The general business groups approached zoning from an economic viewpoint, although this often led them to share the Reformer's ideology. Their economic interest in the city gave them a stake in a "healthy, growing community" where tax rates were not prohibitive, where city government was "efficient," and where some of the problems of the urban environment—a constricting labor force, congestion, and lack of space—were being attacked. When a new zoning proposal was offered, these groups were inclined to test the proposal against these criteria.

Harold Riegelman (of the Citizens Budget Commission): The current zoning is inadequate, and this is made all the more apparent by advances in the philosophy and science of zoning. We need a strong tax base, it is necessary to a healthy city. There should be encouragement to industrial development, especially, particularly through the prohibition of residential construction in existing and future industrial areas.[19]

Traditionally, these groups favored zoning in the abstract, during the 1930s having been some of the more vocal organizations for revision of the "old" 1916 code, especially to eliminate "congestion."[20] At the same time, the Chamber of Commerce, the Citizens Budget Commission, and the Commerce and Industry Association consistently opposed specific zoning proposals which ran counter to their perceived stakes in the urban land economy. They threw their substantial prestige against nonconforming use provisions and performance standards for industry, and the Citizens Budget Commission opposed bulk restrictions on business in Manhattan.

Of the three organizations, the Citizens Budget Commission took the great interest in zoning, in part, perhaps, as a consequence of its role as watchdog over the city government for the business interests, and perhaps also as a function of its membership, which was closely tied to the "local" business interests. Organized in 1932, it grew out of the efforts of the New York Real Estate Board, the Merchants Association, the New York Chamber of Commerce, and the New York Board of Trade to find a solution to the city's budget crisis of the Depression Era. In 1960 it had a membership of 750, composed of financial institutions, manufacturing and retail establishments, as well as a smattering of law firms and real estate firms, with a Manhattan bias in its membership.

The Citizens Budget Commission tended to concentrate on the "purely" economic effects of zoning—the consequences of zoning proposals on the city's land values, tax base, and commercial expansion. In general, it was not friendly to what it considered "radical" departures in zoning policy, especially in 1941 and 1944 when efforts to curb nonconforming uses and the floor areas of downtown Manhattan retailers were proposed.

THE LOCAL BUSINESS GROUPS. For the borough-oriented business groups, zoning was construed in an equivalently specific fashion. The stakes of these groups in zoning were similar to those of the city-wide business groups, but were expressed in terms of the individual boroughs. The struggle was for each borough to maintain or expand its business and industrial base, and the zoning proposals which reflected a tendency to reduce either were met with strong opposition. Space allocations, bulk, and nonconforming use provisions were the major targets of these groups.

And, in the comprehensive proposals, it was the outlying borough organizations who felt the pinch of the changes.

Mr. William Savacool (of the Queens Chamber of Commerce): But in large areas the proposed zoning resolution indicates the intention to displace business and industry from their long-established locations and zone the sites for residential use.[21]

Mr. Howard Swain (Brooklyn Chamber of Commerce): Now, let me call attention to specific problems. For example, we have a firm employing 1000 persons, it has increased growth potential, but it can expand only into what you have zoned as an adjacent residential area. If it can't expand here, it will move.[22]

The Queens Chamber of Commerce, the Bronx Board of Trade, and the Staten Island Chamber of Commerce responded most notably to the proposals affecting industrial space allocations and the threat of nonconforming use restrictions.

The Queens Chamber of Commerce was founded in 1909, and in 1960 it had approximately 1,500 members, almost all of them industrial firms. Its demand for the protection and expansion of industrial areas frequently led to open conflict with the homeowners' groups of the borough. It was "conservative" in its zoning philosophy, regarding the "theoreticians" of the City Planning Commission as a real threat to the health of the borough.

The local retail associations also had a strong economic interest in zoning. These were the local "street," "avenue," or area associations, whose memberships were drawn from the retail merchants of a specific, less-than-borough-wide area. The Avenue of the Americas Association (earlier the Sixth Avenue Association), the Broadway Association, the Twenty-third Street Association, the West of Central Park Association, the Downtown Brooklyn Association were but a few. They were characterized by their special geographic "jurisdictions" and by an intense chauvinism toward their areas.[23]

The most familiar and famous of the "street" associations was the Fifth Avenue Association, formed in 1907. It early undertook an aggressive campaign to include in its membership every merchant (and almost all property owners) on Fifth Avenue and the adjacent areas. Both wealthy and of high prestige, through its position on the "most famous shopping avenue in America," it was able to assert its interests as being in the best interests of the city as a whole.[24] It persistently protected the business interests of its merchant members by fending off "encroachments" of hostile uses and by attempting to "upgrade" the avenue through land use designation, sign control ordinances, and special treatment in the traffic plans. The other local business associations resembled the Fifth Avenue Association. They normally had small but competent permanent staffs, and they focused their attention on the careful nurturing of their specific areas. This resulted in a parochial approach to zoning—the local retail associations showed little concern for the problems of other business areas in the city and concentrated specifically on the proposals that touched their jurisdictions.

The Social Interests [25]

The homeowners' groups saw their stake in zoning as primarily "socially" oriented. Almost without exception the homeowners' groups viewed zoning as a potential source of protection or a menace to the integrity of their residential "neighborhoods." This concern was represented by a strong stake in the use and bulk provisions of the code and, to some extent, the administrative provisions—especially those pertaining to the variance power of the Board of Standards and Appeals (the perennial enemy of these groups).

The particular fear of the homeowners' groups was the invasion of multiple dwellings with the concurrent "downgrading" of their areas; in Queens and Staten Island particularly, a running battle was fought to exclude commercial uses from the peripheries of the residential areas. Just as the local business groups were parochial about their areas, the homeowners' associations were protective about their jurisdictions, which they defended from adverse provisions, and for which they constantly demanded higher use and bulk classifications.

Mr. Henry Reichert (President, Glendale Taxpayers' Association): We have one very serious objection. . . . Glendale predominantly is composed of one- and two-family homes; and has been placed in an R-5 zone. We do not believe that this R-5 zone is protection enough. . . . We are told that R-5 will make it possible for apartment houses, apartment hotels [and other uses] to come into our community. If this is so, we voice very strenuous objection, because we do not want to have apartment houses of this type in our area.[26]

This stake in zoning led the homeowners to be in frequent and direct opposition with the local chambers of commerce, the real estate groups, and the builders' associations, especially in Queens and Staten Island and, to a lesser extent, in Brooklyn— areas where the thrust of shifting and growing populations

generated a demand for new commercial areas and apartment
buildings.

Mr. Louis C. Moser (North Queens Home Owners Association):
I love to hear these builders cry—leave it to them and for a buck
they'll cover every inch of ground. Our people have got to have
light and air. . . . As far as the Board of Appeals [*sic*] is concerned,
we of Queens are not happy. If we howl loud enough they'll put
two gas stations on a block instead of three.[27]

The majority of these groups were characterized by their
transient and volunteer nature, although a number—such as the
Murrary Hill Association formed at the time of the 1916
Resolution to oppose commercial and multiple dwelling con-
struction in the exclusive Manhattan neighborhood, the
Douglaston Civic Association (Queens), and a handful of others
—were active throughout the history of zoning in New York
City.

Unlike the majority of the other organized interest groups,
the homeowners' associations rarely had permanent staffing or
the funds to hire regular paid legal consultants. To a great
extent, these groups depended on after-hours volunteer work
or the efforts of interested housewives to plead their cause
before the governmental agencies.

The local civic associations were separated from the homeowners' groups by only a thin line.[28] The fundamental difference lay in the membership base of the two types of groups,
resulting in a differing set of perceptions of stakes in zoning.
The local civic groups included not only homeowners but
apartment dwellers and local business and professional
people.[29] Often the local civic associations also had a broader
geographical base, including in their concept of "neighborhood" the retail areas adjacent to residential developments.
These organizations attempted to speak for the more general
range of their "community's" problems, although they had a
strong common interest with the homeowners' associations.
They also attempted to "upgrade" their areas, by excluding

obnoxious uses and maintaining the status quo in bulk restrictions. They translated their stakes in zoning into a concern about their narrow geographic area, frequently working hand in hand with homeowners' groups (often with overlapping memberships). These groups—among them the Brooklyn Heights Association, the City Island Civic Association, the Yorkville Civic Council, and the Riverdale Neighborhood and Library Association—like the homeowners, feared the encroachments of large-scale commercial and industrial projects and increased residential density. They were attempting to preserve the old neighborhood virtues.

Mr. Judd (of the Brooklyn Hill Civic Association): We approve of the way your resolution treats our area. The old resolution led to a loss of population. The lack of open space, of light and air, has led to a flight to the suburbs, where people can find those things that are so important.[30]

These groups, like the homeowners' associations, generally depended on volunteer staff aid and voluntary contributions for their organizational needs. A few, however, such as the Riverdale Neighborhood and Library Association, had permanent staffs (although often part-time or very small in number).

The Ideological Interests [31]

The groups that were associated with various aspects of municipal reform came closest to having an entirely ideological interest in zoning policy. These were the "general civic groups," "good government" organizations, the groups that acted as the "watchdogs" of the city's government. Chief among them were the City Club, the Citizens Union, the Womens City Club, the Citizens Housing and Planning Council, and the Regional Plan Association.

All were organized to promote the cause of "good government" or some related activity (such as planning and housing), and all were notable for their close attention to the details of the machinery of the city government. Oriented toward an "honest, efficient, and representative" governing of the city, they, through their staffs and committee systems, maintained a constant contact with the city officials. They acted as extra-governmental critics and propagandizers. Their memberships were largely drawn from the middle-class, professional class segments of the city's population, and depended heavily on volunteer labor in report writing, fact gathering, and public appearances.

The Citizens Housing and Planning Council and the Regional Plan Association had a strong bias in favor of the planning ideology, the latter having been formed and led in its early years by members of the 1914–16 Zoning Commissions.

The Citizens Union, formed just prior to the turn of the century, began as a political party and then went through a gradual metamorphosis into an interest group. More frequently concerned with supervising the rules of the game than focusing on particular policy issues, the Citizens Union nevertheless was a constant advocate of "progressive, modernized" zoning. It normally favored the proposals of the City Planning Commission, although it advanced suggestions of its own—usually in the direction of a "harder," more restrictive policy.

These groups were active proponents of the ideological goals of city planning and, in their roles as watchdogs and Reformers, approached most nearly the status of a friendly constituency for the City Planning Commission. Nonetheless, they were selective in offering their support for the commission's proposals, and zoning in the city was rarely a major focus of their activities. The Regional Plan Association was more concerned with planning for the metropolitan area as a whole, the Citizens Housing and Planning Council more interested in the intricacies of public housing and urban renewal, and the Citizens Union and the City Club had sufficient commitment to other aspects of the city's government to draw much of their attention from the technicalities of zoning policy-making.

These organizations turned their attention to the form and structure of the zoning proposals, examining them for internal consistency, conformance with the "principles of good planning," and concessions to the "special interests." [32] Typically, the general civic groups were impatient with the ineffectiveness of the City Planning Commission in its political environment and sought a more centralized method of administering and controlling the Zoning Resolution.

In recent years (since 1956), the older Reform organizations have been partly eclipsed by the activities of the Reform Democrats. The Reform Democrats systematically turned their attention to winning control of the regular Democratic machinery. After bitter struggles in Greenwich Village, the West Side, and other areas of the city, they achieved a large measure of success. The new Reform Democrat clubs consistently were more concerned with the fascinating game of party politics than the more technical and mundane world of policy formulation. Nevertheless, their efforts, and their growing power, helped to set the stage for Mayor Wagner's support of the 1960 zoning proposal. In all probability, Wagner's growing identification with the Reform clubs enabled him to identify more closely with a Reform-oriented program such as comprehensive zoning. The new Reformers, moreover, helped to give voice to the traditional Reform slogans of efficient, economic, and comprehensive city government. The alliance was partly intellectual, but it was also partly an extension of the older Reform movements under Mitchel and La Guardia that had helped upset the form of government.

One further set of nongovernmental participants must be mentioned: the press.[33] While the newspapers in the city are large landholders, the role of the press was not quite like that of any of the other nongovernmental actors. The press was in part one of the referees of the rules of the game, especially the informal rules—calling attention to what it considered violations. It was also an access point to the governmental agencies. In these two respects it was more or less neutral. The newspapers, however, rarely allowed zoning matters to pass without taking a positive stand on the issue.

Generally the city-wide newspapers favored the ideological propositions of zoning and almost as often the specific provisions of particular proposals. In the 1959–60 controversy, for example, only the *Journal-American* showed hesitation toward the proposals. A search of the files of the major metropolitan newspapers for the period of the principal zoning proposals will show, however, a tendency of the press to run parallel to the general civic groups in their assessments of the issues. This is not to suggest that these groups "dominated" the press, which would be patently untrue, but rather that the stake of the press tended to be similar—that of the generalized, comprehensive overseer of the zoning controversy. The nature of zoning as news also affected the reaction of the newspapers. As one real estate reporter said:

You must keep in mind that zoning is apt to be news when it is seen as the struggle of the general interest against the real estate moguls. Couched in these terms it has public interest, otherwise it may be too technical to be worth covering. The big coverage that the 1960 plan got, which is more than any other, I think, except perhaps in 1916, was from this reason. And the papers don't want to take a stand that will make them appear to be for the "special" interests, for the landlords and the exploiters, whatever the private views of the editors, reporters, or columnists may be.

The other participants, both governmental and nongovernmental, considered a "good" press vital to their cause, and many of the activities of both segments were concerned with preparing the ground for reporting in the newspapers. Generally, it was the New York *Times* that gave the greatest editorial and news coverage to the zoning proposals, and the *Times* most consistently favored the efforts of the proponents of zoning.

Group Resources

Each interest group brought some resources to the zoning contest: the general business groups, their prestige and connections in the worlds of finance, industry, and government, and their large staffs; the real estate and architects' groups, an intimate involvement in land use policies and a professional competence in the field; the general civic groups, their political skill and knowledge from years of being in the political arena; and the homeowners' and local civic groups, their more or less mass memberships.

All but the last two groupings had professional staffs who could analyze problems, write reports, and attend hearings. Most of the organizations had legal counsel, either as voluntary members or on a consultant basis.[34]

At the same time, it is difficult, if not impossible, to assess the relative "strengths" of the nongovernmental interest groups in the zoning contest. Few, if any, were totally cohesive, few had the opportunity or inclination to devote their full time and efforts to any given zoning controversy, all operated within the confines of a more or less limited view of the zoning arena. Further, all were represented in the policial contest by individuals—their leaders or spokesmen—and this introduced the incalculable aspect of personality, skill, and individual behavior. Obviously the individual leader could be a resource of positive benefit for the group's aims, or he could be a critical hindrance.[35]

Certainly one of the major resources that can be brought to a political contest is a solid front. So far, a great deal of emphasis has been placed on the elements of division within the interest group population: the limits and difference among stakes and interests and the conflicts (or at least the gaps) that arose among the representatives of these differing viewpoints.

Efforts were made not only to bring cohesion within functional groupings of related occupations or interests but to span

several concerns. Usually, these attempts were of limited duration and of only small binding power.

The Metropolitan Real Estate Boards Association was an
example of one of these efforts, but it had only limited success
in bringing cohesion to the real estate community, on zoning
questions at any rate. The same applies to the Architects Council. In Queens the giant Federation of Civic Councils, claiming
200 homeowners' organizations and approximately 180,000 out
of 260,000 one- and two-family homeowners, was a similar alliance. It was formed in 1956 to avoid clashes between its associated members. It nevertheless permitted full autonomy in
"local" matters to its member groups.

One of the weaknesses of these peak associations was that
their cohesive ability depended on the congruence of interests
of their members. They did not have the ability (or perhaps
the desire) to apply meaningful sanctions to wayward members. They were confederations and the most that they could
withhold from a dissenter was their support: a relatively idle
threat to an independently based group such as the New York
Real Estate Board or the New York Chapter of the American
Institute of Architects.[36]

Related to but separate from these "permanent" alliances
were the occasional *ad hoc* peak associations which grew out
of a response to a particular zoning proposal. The most significant of these—the Save New York Committee (1916), the Citizens Zoning Committee (1944 and 1949–52), and the Committee for Modern Zoning (1959–60)—are worth noting because
they represented efforts that were more "successful" than similar endeavors to bring a broadly based cohesion to the fragmented interest group population, and all were formed purely
in response to the issues of zoning.

Other efforts to achieve cohesiveness within the nongovernmental zoning population won only moderate success. Patterns
of informal alliances appeared, for example, in Staten Island

during 1959 and early 1960 between the Chamber of Commerce, the local real estate board, and the Homebuilders Association. In Queens, the Chamber of Commerce was able to build a temporary alliance with a small number of homeowners' groups. In both cases, however, the alliances did not last for the duration of the struggle. One actor said:

Few organizations had that much in common. You have to remember that all of them had their separate problems, separate goals. If one reached the point where he was getting satisfaction, he would simply terminate his relationship with his erstwhile friends.

Or as another participant put it:

You try to find friends where you can if you think you're losing. If you're winning, you don't really care. And the fact is, none of these things [alliances] ever manage to last very long. It's not in the nature of the situation, or the nature of the groups involved.

Another force moving toward either general or specialized cohesion, however, was that of overlapping memberships. While the complex web of group affiliations defies any ready description, interlocking directorates, multiple memberships, and joint leaderships were sufficiently frequent to indicate that there were bases for common action lying parallel to or within the composition of the formal and informal alliances.[37] The Fifth Avenue Association, for example, fostered a number of similar organizations within its jurisdiction, and the members of these groups were all members of the association.[38] Further, the Fifth Avenue Association and the New York Real Estate Board, the Broadway Association, and the Citizens Budget Commission all have had common members.[39] In Brooklyn, the pattern of interlocking directorates appeared in the 1959–60 controversy within the civic associations, while in the Bronx, the same man acted as the spokesman for the Bronx Real Estate Board and the Bronx Board of Trade.[40] Often groups with such close-knit ties shared common interests and stakes in zoning.

At the same time, the multiple affiliations of individuals did not necessarily lead to any complete linkage among groups.[41]

One active group member and leader said:

Most prominent civic leaders belong to a large number of organizations. But what it may look like on paper is not also reflective of actual conditions in real life. Sometimes you belong to a group for very personal reasons—business reasons, or your wife feels it is the thing to do, or your friends who belong have persuaded you. A lot of these fellows are carried on the rolls and pay their dues and never show up or do any work. And if they did, if they did come to meetings, it might be just to object to what the club or the organization has been doing.

Nevertheless, within the context of the political struggle, there may often be present the raw materials for building up the kind of *ad hoc* group that appeared in the form of the Save New York Committee or the Citizens Zoning Committee.

The resources and linkages of the groups become meaningful, however, only in terms of their relations and interactions with the governmental participants in the zoning contest, for it is in these relations that the claims were pressed upon the process of implementing the zoning proposals.

The local groups—retail merchants, homeowners, civic associations—all tended to have a more or less close working relationship with the borough president of their respective boroughs. The broad membership bases of the homeowners' and local civic groups commanded the attention of the borough president when he was aroused to action.[42] The same appeared to apply to the mayor—he would lend his ear to what appeared to be a ground swell of grass-roots opinion. Simultaneously, however, the local business groups and the borough and local real estate boards also had a basis for an appeal to the borough president. Their close link to the economic livelihood of the borough placed them in a strategic position to speak authoritatively about the threat of zoning to the well-being of the borough. Moreover, the real estate boards worked closely with the borough presidents in the mutual areas of public works and physical maintenance. Their relations with the borough presidents were day-to-day and routinized, and often the real estate boards sprang to the defense of the prerogatives and diminishing responsibilities of the borough presidents.

The general civic associations self-consciously maintained a tie with the agencies of the city government—a practical necessity for them to perform their self-appointed tasks of criticism, observation, and information gathering and dissemination. The Citizens Union, for one, had a multiplicity of committees that carefully went over and reported on practically every aspect of the government of the city. To be able to perform this task, its staff members attended hearings and conferred on a regular basis with governmental officials.

With the gradual encroachment on the responsibilities of the borough presidents in zoning matters, the focus of activity shifted toward the City Planning Commission and the mayor's office, at least in comprehensive zoning matters. Liaison with both was considered vital by many of the groups and was carefully tended.[43] Nevertheless, the joint informal rules of the game—for example, borough courtesy and the cult of unanimity—served to preserve the role of the borough president in the contest and as a focus of interest for group activity.

Summary

Just as the stakes of the governmental actors in the zoning system tended to structure the orientations of the governmental agencies toward zoning, so the stakes and interests of the nongovernmental actors affected the reactions of the interest groups toward zoning.

The numerous and diverse nongovernmental actors represented economic, social, and ideological interests in the zoning system. The economic interests—the building groups, real estate groups, architects' groups, and city-wide and local business groups—tended to focus on the provisions of zoning proposals that would affect their specific stakes. The builders, realtors, and architects were primarily concerned with provisions affecting building bulk and nonconforming uses. The business groups were concerned most often with use provisions, while the city-wide business groups took a more general view of zoning as public policy.

The social interests—homeowners and local civic groups— felt themselves to be most affected by use or bulk provisions that touched on their particular neighborhoods.

The Reform groups represented the ideological interest in zoning. These organizations approached zoning from the viewpoint of defenders of the public interest and watchdogs of the city government.

Characteristically, divisions appeared under each of the major categories of interests and stakes. The groups representing the "big" architects or "big" realtors rarely agreed with the organizations representing their less famous or smaller colleagues. Even where there was no direct conflict, interests generally were not congruent, and groups tended to focus on their local or specific problems and areas. The pattern was one of fragmentation and specialization.

Each category of interest groups brought related resources to the zoning system. The economic interests had the advantage of their prestige and familiarity with the land economy of the city; the social interests had their mass memberships, and the ideological or Reform groups their expertise in the operations of the city's government as well as easy access to the press.

VI

PROCESSES AND STRATEGIES

Each participant in the zoning system has had to accept as relatively stable determinants its own group interests and the rules of the game. Although these factors might shift over a period of time—the Citizens Union, for example, changed from a political party to a civic "watchdog"; the Reform groups modified the rules of the game by establishing the City Planning Commission—when the participants worked within the context of a single zoning issue, these long-run forces were largely outside the control of the individual participants.

The functioning of the zoning system was even more complex than the foregoing discussion would suggest, however. Although the initial reactions of the participants were strongly shaped by their stakes in zoning, and available lines of action were limited by the rules of the game, the zoning system was also structured by its general characteristics, and within the envelope of these characteristics, certain strategies and processes appeared that operated to modify the pattern of fragmentation and noncongruence of interests.

The General Characteristics of the Zoning System

The zoning system was "middle class" in style. Of the groups appearing in the zoning struggles, only a few were representative of the underprivileged, unpropertied, and the economically or socially disadvantaged.[1] When the Planning Commission or the First and Second Zoning Commissions talked of "grass-roots" support they referred primarily to the organized homeowners, not to such "newcomers" as the Negroes, Puerto Ricans, organized or unorganized tenant groupings, or other similar social or economic groupings.[2]

The "middle-class" character of zoning gave it its own style; although persuasion and propaganda played significant roles, these were rarely demagogic. There were "demonstrations"—in 1940, 1944–45, and in 1960—but these were "orderly" and, when they began to shade toward disorderliness, the other actors frowned on them. One of the informal rules of the game appeared to be gentlemanly behavior. As one interest group leader said:

There are ways and ways of doing things. Generally, in zoning, the press, the public officials, other organizations are embarrassed, or even angry, if an organization misbehaves. There was a Queens group that forced its way into a public hearing and was raising a rumpus; this was just embarrassing and did not help their cause. It created a great deal of misunderstanding in fact.

The homeowners persistently addressed themselves to the problem of keeping "undesirables" out of their neighborhoods, but there were no spokesmen for these undesirables—except when the undesirable elements were owners of filling stations or multistory buildings. Zoning is not per se discriminatory, but some kinds of political behavior were excluded from the zoning system. The "middle-class" nature of zoning put an emphasis on certain political and behavior patterns: persuasion, bargaining, rationality, and organized, staffed activity. Demagoguery, efforts to give a voice to the "unorganized," mass demonstrations, and the application of pressure through violence or disorderly behavior were deemphasized or totally prohibited. Zoning issues appeared as lukewarm rather than high temperature politics.

The issues of zoning put a priority on technical expertise.

Although activity in the zoning arena did not belong solely to those with high technical competence—the planners, lawyers, engineers, and architects—consistently the other actors depended on these professional services to vocalize their claims before governmental agencies; and within the agencies of government, the lawyers, planners, and engineers had a near monopoly of the advice-giving functions. Bassett and McAneny were lawyers in both training and background, Purdy was a tax expert; the first two Zoning Commissions had a heavy representation of architects, lawyers, and engineers. During the 1920s and 1930s, lawyers and engineers handled the greater part of zoning matters in the borough presidents' offices and before the Board of Standards and Appeals (which was itself composed of members of these professions). The Planning Commission, while by no means dominated by the "expert" professions, had its share of these professional groupings. And the staff of the Planning Commission, by charter requirement, was made up of engineers, planners, architects, and, in a few cases, lawyers.

Part of the emphasis on technical know-how came from the very nature of zoning as public policy. It would be an imprudent layman who attempted to understand fully the complexities and legalities of a contemporary zoning proposal. Even the real estate boards, who worked with the substance of zoning in their daily activities, relied heavily on lawyers and architects to act as their representatives in zoning issues; and this was equally true of other nongovernmental interest groups.

There was another kind of expertise involved, however, in addition to technical skills: political expertise. Although it is difficult to gather data on the actors who found themselves partially or totally excluded from the zoning system from lack of knowing how to "get around" in politics, there is some evidence to indicate that groups without experienced professional staffs, or who did not participate frequently in political activity, were at a loss in their attempts to assert their zoning claims. In a number of cases groups were content with appearing at public hearings or writing letters to the Planning Commission. The response to an interviewer's questions as to why they did not attempt to appeal to members of the Board of Estimate or why they did not attempt to find political allies indicated that apparently some had just not thought of the process in these terms.[3] Although a Bassett or a Felt might actively try to seek out such groups, on the whole these actors seemed to be more or less unable to participate competently— their claims were just not heard. In the words of one group spokesman:

It took us nearly a year to learn that we had to find our own way around. The only way to be listened to was to find out whom we had to speak to. We started by writing one letter to the mayor and thought we had done our job. But then some of us went to a public hearing, after we had missed the first round of informal hearings, and found that more experienced people were doing a lot more— so we started making phone calls, asking for conferences with the city planners, and so forth.[4]

Linkages: 1913–1938

The general characteristics of the zoning system—its middle-class nature, the emphasis on political and technical know-how —served to constrict the outer boundaries of the system. Although the system did not preclude actors who were eager to learn and willing to go through the hard process of gaining a place on the stage, it was shaped by these limiting factors.

Within the zoning system itself, however, there were processes which operated to create lesser subsystems, linking a group's interests with the activities of other participants and creating internal patterns of behavior within the larger system. Often these processes were dependent on the strategies of the participants in a particular zoning issue; often they were dependent on the structure of the rules of the game or the location of the group within the context of the system; and often they appeared to be dependent on mutual interests and alignments on zoning questions.

Prior to 1938 and the introduction of the Planning Commission into the zoning arena, the basic linkage of interests was centered around the borough presidents' offices and the Board of Standards and Appeals, with the Democratic party organizations acting as brokers. This state of affairs stemmed from two factors: first, the structural features of the system—the inherent localism of the situation; and second, the processes that McAneny and Bassett used to win passage of the 1916 Resolution. There was formal recognition of the importance of borough interests in the Committee on City Planning, and, in the process of winning the support of both governmental agencies and local interests, the first resolution represented an initial linking of the agencies of government—especially the borough engineers, the building superintendents, and the BSA —with the nongovernmental interests. In combination with the informal rule of borough courtesy on the Board of Estimate and the highly localized nature of most interests, the product was a symbiotic relation between the borough president and the local interest group. The builders, the real estate men, and the developers had to work with the borough engineers in the course of their daily activities and the Zoning Resolution of 1916 only reinforced this tendency. A strong link was thus built between Borough Hall and the local economic groups, a link that perhaps redounded to the advantage of those with technical and political expertise, but that was also, at its level, apparently satisfactory to most of the parties concerned. The borough president was able to maintain a close contact with local building activity, the political party organizations (both within and outside the borough presidency) had a working contact with important constituency groups, and the local groups found the way smoothed for the pursuit of their activities.

To a limited extent, the same process of interaction seemed to apply to the relation between the borough president's office and the homeowners' groups, with the exception that these groups were more concerned with blocking action than with promoting favorable building conditions; as a consequence they often stood in opposition to the interests of the builders and realtors.

A major characteristic of the process in the period 1913 to 1938 was that it was primarily "vertical" rather than "horizontal." The evidence suggests that very rarely did groups find common cause and form alliances. The pattern of relations was almost entirely bilateral: between group and borough office. In part this stemmed from the localism of most groups: organizations that were separated spatially or in their interests had little reason to ally. And economic groups were often competitive with each other for the limited space available: builders, gas station owners, and homeowners in Queens or Staten Island had small reason to join forces. Further, the fact that the approach to the Zoning Resolution was piecemeal gave little impetus for similar interests to combine on a wide front: local applications or amendments of the zoning code could arouse only local interests.

The same pattern applied to the Board of Standards and Appeals. Although more "city-wide" than the borough offices (in the sense that it was administering the resolution with the whole city as its jurisdiction), the BSA built a set of tightly knit interactions with a fairly select group of those in the building industry and in the architectural professions. But, once again, the important linkages were vertical rather than horizontal.

The role of the party organizations in this system can be underestimated. While the party clubhouses could not bring union among conflicting interests, they did work to dampen overt conflict among competing groups. In the policy-neutral and prudent manner characteristic of party leaders, the local Democratic organizations were apparently unwilling to handle controversial zoning questions—their sanction was to refuse to give the borough president the "go ahead" on the Board of Estimate until a nongovernmental settlement had been reached. By no means successful in all cases, this process inhibited the carrying of conflicts into the governmental arena and encouraged informal nongovernmental decisions.[5]

During the period 1917–38, then, the pattern was one of linkages between the borough president and local groups and between the BSA and local groups, with the party acting as mediator and expediter. The Board of Estimate was primarily a means of ratifying decisions made at lower governmental (or nongovernmental) levels, and there was little formal or informal interaction among interest groups except in conflict situations.

A major feature of this pattern was that the general, city-wide, planning and ideology-oriented groups were omitted from the process. Zoning was carried on as a matter of local concern, a process of decision making that involved local interests, the local party organizations, and governmental agencies with local orientations. At no point was the "city-wide," "efficient," and "rational" Reformer's model of the city represented. It is clear that the Merchants Association, the Regional Plan Association, the Citizens Union, the City Club, and, later, the Citizens Budget Commission were well aware of this omission. Although the city-wide members of the Board of Estimate were possible sources of representation for these groups, the close ties of the mayor, comptroller, and the president of the Board of Aldermen to the county and local organizations of the party meant only frustration for the "broad" view. The city-wide organizations turned to Walker in 1929 in an effort to get a planning agency—a body that would presumably represent their concerns—but the veto efforts of the borough presidents and their allies resulted in a compromise that was unsatisfactory to the Reform-oriented.

The only hope of the ideological groups was to break the ongoing equilibrium. The success of Reform-Fusion at the polls with La Guardia, and the promise of charter revision, gave these groups their opportunity. The establishment of a Planning Commission, even though it involved compromises recognizing borough autonomy, was a major break in the processes and linkages of the 1920s and 1930s. The Planning Commission's "independence" from partisan influence and borough concerns would be, it was hoped, the instrument for the representation of the "city-wide" interests and the supporters of those interests.

The Post–1938 Processes

After the creation of the Planning Commission, one could have anticipated the development of a coalition between the new agency and such city-wide groups as the Regional Plan Association, the Citizens Union, and the City Club. The zoning process would have become one in which these groups worked closely together to formulate and implement their model of the city, while the older blocs of borough president, local group, and the BSA would have been only weakly counterpoised against the Reform coalition. The expected pattern did not develop but the traditional one did go into decline.

Although the Planning Commission did receive some support from the civic groups in its early struggles, the linkage became increasingly tenuous. Part of this was due to the nature of the groups themselves: most of the Reform-oriented groups were more concerned with governmental procedures than with the actual substance of policy. These groups won their victory when the Planning Commission was established. What the commission did with itself was to a large measure its own concern; the Reform groups could feel their interests had been

represented. Further, when the commission failed, the tendency
of the city-wide groups was merely to become impatient with
its ineptitude. Their concern with electoral politics, or the
details of budget procedures and civil service processes, meant
that many of these groups were limited in the scope of their
interests—staffs could be spread only so thin, volunteer memberships could sacrifice only so much time from the demands
of their professions. The troubles of the Planning Commission
came low on this list of priorities.

The groups themselves were of sufficiently different interests
and internal needs to make a coalition among them difficult.
Although capable of working together for limited periods of
time, the Reform-oriented groups seemed destined to go their
separate ways most of the time.

The Planning Commission itself was not in a position to
cultivate the kind of broad-based support that it needed. Unlike the governmental actors in the older system, it functioned
in a radically different style: it did not operate on the principle
of "helping matters along" and thus created a mutually bene-
ficial and closely linked relationship with those who turned to it
on zoning problems. Instead, the commission weighed the
merits of zoning requests on the basis of the planning model it
was charged with instead of the favor-given, favor-received process of the 1917–38 system. Although the Zoning Resolution was
amended—practically as many amendments were made in the
twenty-two years after the establishment of the Planning Commission as in the twenty-two years before—these amendments
did not create a friendly constituency-agency pattern; instead,
there was a purely formal processing of amendments on their
individual merits.

Thus the advent of the Planning Commission drastically
modified the older system. The interposition of the commission
as a third force, one which was primarily responsible for the
initial processing and recommending of zoning changes, tended

to break down the pattern of borough president and interest group relations. The "independence" of the commission, moreover, freed it from the embarrassment of phone calls from the borough presidents to "move things along," and groups found it increasingly meaningless to appeal either to the borough president or to the local party organization in zoning matters.

The role of the BSA changed after 1932 under the leadership of Harris Murdock. Although Murdock built a close working relation with building and real estate groups, it was a limited one. Murdock, through his interpretation of the Zoning Resolution and perhaps because the Planning Commission was an ever present threat to the discretionary powers of the BSA, administered the resolution faithfully to the letter of the law.

The changing role of the party also affected the functioning of the zoning system. The evolving environment of party politics, and the changed pattern of relations between interest groups and the borough offices in zoning matters, increasingly excluded the party organization as a broker in the system. An apparent indication of this is that conflicts between competing groups were brought with greater frequency into the governmental arena—the code continued to change, but the processes of settlement had been modified.[6]

Processes and Strategies: 1913–1938

The basic political tactics of the zoning system—propaganda, bargaining, alliance building, applying pressure through phone calls, letters, and other such activities—are typical of the behavior of interest groups throughout the city.[7] But there have been differences in the general shape of the strategic processes relied on by the major participants of the zoning system, with 1938 serving as the dividing point for these differences.

For the period before 1938, the pattern was one in which nongovernmental participants and the governmental actors dealing with them operated on the basis of a low commitment to any absolutist interpretation of zoning. Zoning as a "city-wide" or comprehensive policy was less significant than the stability of the system and the immediate problems confronting the participants. Bargaining was usually a parochial, *quid pro quo* arrangement. The emphasis was on informality and, as far as the processes of zoning were concerned, there was only a thin dividing line between the agencies of government and the nongovernmental groups in formulating the content of zoning policy.

Thus the Fifth Avenue Association turned to McAneny in 1911 and 1912 because it found that it was unable to solve the problem of the invading lofts alone. When Bassett, Purdy, and McAneny undertook the larger task of building a comprehensive zoning ordinance for the city, the Fifth Avenue Association (apparently by mutual agreement) was represented on the First and Second Zoning Commissions. Included also in these commissions were the representatives of the architectural, engineering, real estate, and business professions— all interests who would most probably be affected by the zoning proposals.

This was shrewd political strategy by McAneny and Bassett. By placing these groups on the Zoning Commissions they ensured their own access to the interests involved; they had two-way lines of communication and, by winning agreement from the representatives of key interests early in the game, they simplified their task of mustering general support for the proposals. Bassett and McAneny had, however, also ensured that these groups would be participants in the process of formulating and publicizing the code. In effect, the Resolution of 1916 was largely a product of the interest group constituency of zoning. The Fifth Avenue Association virtually wrote the provisions for its area, as apparently did other groups for theirs. Bassett and McAneny came to zoning with few prior commitments; their intention was to ameliorate what they saw as certain obvious evils in the physical composition of the city as it then existed, but they were uncertain as to what the final product of the zoning process should be. One who knew Bassett described the way the code was formulated:

He saw the problem as one of imposing restrictions, certainly. But he also felt that certain concessions had to be made for each restriction, that those who were concerned with their problems on a daily basis had the right to concretely shape the solution to those problems.

Bassett and McAneny also achieved a joining of the governmental interests in the Zoning Resolution. The borough presidents, the building superintendents, and other less vital agents were represented in the final formulation of the plan. The strategy boiled down to this: *given* that a zoning resolution was to be formulated, all concerned interests must be represented. The crucial stage for Bassett and McAneny was winning the "given." The process of writing a proposal was then one of working closely with as many interests as possible. Winning a general acceptance of zoning was achieved in much the same fashion as the final formulation of the plan—by a careful articulation and representation of groups and their interests. The major failure of this strategy was in Staten Island, where, apparently through oversight or geographical problems, the Zoning Commissions failed to gain the support of the local groups in the Island.

The Save New York Committee, which briefly emerged as a threat to the 1916 zoning plan, became instead a parallel and contributing movement. No overt alliance was made with this *ad hoc* movement; it worked in an area that Bassett considered legally impossible and McAneny probably considered politically unwise for the Zoning Commission to handle. But since it was apparently closely joined to the zoning movement, it had the effect of reinforcing the Zoning Commission's position—the Save New York Committee could apply sanctions that the official Zoning Commission could not.

The techniques of rational persuasion, face-to-face negotiation, seeking out nonrepresented groups, and balancing conflicting claims were all patterned (either consciously or intuitively) to make the strategy effective. Bassett and McAneny appear to have relied on bargaining as a means of permitting groups to express their claims in exchange for their support for the general premise of zoning as such. At heart, it was a process of flexible pragmatism.

This strategy was carried to its logical extension in the 1920s and 1930s. Its weakness perhaps was that it relied fundamentally on the localism and plurality of interests, both governmental and nongovernmental, and, when developed into a consistent process, it excluded the general, city-wide groups. Its strength was that it required little in the way of counter-strategies on the part of the zoning constituency; and because it maximized the representation of local interests, there was little reason for these groups to search for ways to fight zoning qua zoning. Conflicts arose only over specific applications of the code in highly specific areas. The accommodation of local interests localized conflicts.

The Strategies of Alliance Building: 1938–1960

The interposition of the Planning Commission destroyed the equilibrium that had been established as an outgrowth of the 1916 Resolution. Strategically, the Planning Commission occupied the embarrassing position of being dependent on the stakes and interests of other governmental agencies for the passage of its plans, without having friendly interest groups surrounding it as a resource to bring pressure to bear at critical times. The Charter, the leadership, and the staff of the commission also gave it a high commitment to the ideological bases of zoning; the commission shared with the general civic groups a concept of zoning as an instrument of comprehensiveness, of a "general model" of the city, of rationality and efficiency. In effect, this meant that there was a hard core beyond which Tugwell, or even Moses, was unwilling to bargain, an unwillingness shared by Orton during the HB&A struggle. Bassett and McAneny, Reformer-like, had been primarily concerned with zoning per se, as a process that should be enacted into law, and the policy content was not of primary importance to them. But what they passed on was a process that excluded the general civic groups and a policy area in which content became of critical importance to city planners.

Tugwell took an unbending stance, which not only generated opposition but which tended to prohibit his searching out interest group support or finding means of dividing the opposition. The image of the "general interest" provided little room for the accommodation of "special interests."

The Moses plan was more flexible, and the resource of Moses' magic name brought support to the proposal that Tugwell could not find for his. Yet, as the strength of the support for the plan increased, the tendency toward counter-maneuver also increased. Robert Dowling's 1944 Citizens Zoning Committee came into being, an alliance founded on the mutual interests of groups threatened by the cutback in bulk. The Planning Commission, through La Guardia, was willing to bargain to a limited extent, but this was without having sought out the representation or the desires of the realtors, retailers, and trade groups that were the major elements of the Citizens Zoning Committee. The CZC opted to refuse negotiation and turned instead to the formal rules of the game for its winning strategic combination.

During the HB&A controversy of 1949–52, Finkelstein moved toward building some sort of workable combination of interests joined to the Planning Commission, but when he was not reappointed to office this effort went by the board. The commission, with Orton acting as spokesman, once again took a relatively uncompromising position early enough in the development of the issue to make the proposal a threat rather than an opportunity for most interests. At the same time that the commission was failing to build any sort of workable alliance, Latham Squire relied on the peak association of the realtors and the Board of Standards and Appeals to build an informal bloc of opposition to the proposal. Even so, Squire indicated a willingness to bargain on the condition that the realtors, builders, and other economic groups were represented in the process of formulating the amendments, but the Planning Commission was unwilling to enter the process on those terms.

James Felt found a workable equivalent for what Bassett and McAneny had relied upon. The existence of the Planning Commission and its staff prevented the establishment of a Zoning Commission of the type Bassett and McAneny created —such a tactic would have been a blow to the morale of the organization that Felt had built up—but he was able to establish the Committee for Modern Zoning. Felt himself acted as a further means of access to the real estate and financial communities, while his staff, utilized to the fullest, provided a means of creating and maintaining almost constant contact with the possible sources of opposition or support in the field.

Felt, moreover approached the zoning amendment from the view of winning a victory, almost without regard to policy content. Like Bassett and McAneny, Felt saw the critical point as the process of winning, not the final product of the process. Although Felt's staff and allies found this a distasteful approach to the ideology of planning, it allowed Felt to assume a position in which bargaining was simplified—almost any concession was permissible that would win the support needed to get a unanimous vote on the Board of Estimate. There were, however, some restraints operating on Felt—in all likelihood he was aware that the bargaining process could be carried only so far without alienating the general civic groups—so bargaining was used primarily as a means of winning the support of the homeowners and the limited segments of the business, real estate, and building communities. All of these were amenable to specific terms of negotiation. Those groups—the Brooklyn, Bronx, and Queens Real Estate Boards, the Queens Chamber of Commerce—that took an inflexible stand were omitted from the process; since they could be sufficiently isolated by oceans of grass-roots support and the key elements of the Manhattan real estate and financial world, their opposition was overcome.

Felt relied on a strategy of division—one in which organized (or potentially organizable) opposition was destroyed piece by piece. At the same time, the counterstrategy of the opposition, to find allies and to generate a solid front, foundered on the loss of its principal strategist and the resulting tactical sluggishness.

Felt, moreover, had built his own alliances: with the mayor, with the Committee on Modern Zoning, and by relying on his personal connections in the real estate community. As the struggle wore on, his ability to bargain successfully for support was simplified as support snowballed. Finally he was able to break the real estate boards' alliance, the Architects Council, and the Staten Island business-realtor bloc.

The period from 1938 to 1960 was generally characterized by strategies in which the greatest emphasis was placed on finding temporary functional equivalents for the patterns of the previous twenty-two years. The nongovernmental groups usually were favorable to zoning in principle if they were to be allowed a hand in negotiating the concrete terms of the amendments; the Planning Commission more often than not took a position of all-or-nothing; concessions on comprehensive proposals were to be limited if any concessions at all were to be granted. The nongovernmental groups, blocked from representation in the process of writing the code, were forced to turn to a strategy of finding the necessary support to veto commission proposals through alliance building.

Under Felt, the Planning Commission itself turned to a parallel set of techniques: by operating first from a predisposition to bargain and then with the intent of building its own constituency and allies while dividing the opposition, the commission was able to give interest groups a part in remodeling the consultants' proposals and thus find the key to victory before the Board of Estimate.

But the two eras in the history of the politics of zoning differed considerably. The first period (1913–38) was marked by one of low commitments to general policy content, with the concomitant that bargaining was easy and informal and approached cooperation more closely than it did conflict. The major structural feature of the process—localism—was less an obstacle that had to be overcome than an asset that could be used to dampen overt conflict and thus increase the stability of the system.

The second period (post-1938) saw a major reorientation. For the Planning Commission, at least, policy content was an important commitment. The disruption of the older system resulted in a fluidity that required alliances cutting across interests to either pass or block a zoning proposal. Localism had to be overcome if the actors were to hope for success.

But the early efforts to overcome localism were only temporary, and no functional equivalent to the older symbiotic system appeared. Felt, by turning the localism of the system to his advantage as a means to split his opposition, was able to win a victory, but this also appears to have been only a temporary and limited success.

The Processes of Bargaining: Two Cases

Bargaining was a core process in the zoning system. It was not necessarily the only means by which groups represented their claims on zoning policy, for actors may refuse to enter bargaining negotiations in the hope that one of their other maneuvers might save them from having to make concessions.

In the zoning system, however, bargaining provided the principal way through which the actors avoided total defeat or asserted their interests.

Success in bargaining depended on many variables; the commitment of the protagonists to their respective goals, the degree of conflict among goals, the availability of alternatives, and the apparent or real strength of one of the actors all affected who bargained and with what degree of success.[8] Citing two instances may help to clarify this line of argument.

A leader of a homeowners' group who requested anonymity discussed a bargaining process during the 1959–60 struggle in the following terms:

We were faced with an uncomfortable position [in the spring of 1960]. In general the plan seemed good, but a lot of our people were unhappy with it. When we held a meeting, a lot of the members said we should go to the hearings and protest because we were not getting sufficient protection.

Apparently many of those who "were being hurt" lived on the periphery of the neighborhood and were already seeing apartments being built which might house "undesirable elements." The leader was vague as to the proportion of the membership opposed to the plan and whether he shared their views. He was elected president, incidentally, of the group on a year-by-year basis and was a practicing attorney with his offices near his place of residence.

I called up one of the fellows at the Planning Department that I knew about and we discussed it. He said he would like to get together with us. We talked about the matter a great deal with him. Basically what we wanted was a new use district—higher than the one the plan put us in. We explained our situation. He [the planner] showed us why we were in the district that we were in and how it fitted into his figures and projections and so forth and I could see his point. . . . But I said I would have to talk to some of the other people in our association. When I did they were still not very happy. I called the planner back up and we discussed it some more. He explained that he had gone over our problem and had decided that we could be upgraded but we would still have to stay in the same use category. We dickered about it and I finally hinted that we would have to withhold our endorsement of the plan unless we got the higher district.

At this point, the leader and the planner apparently conferred about the developing situation.

[The planner] pointed out that it looked very like the proposal would go through as it was and we could either go through with the change he had offered us or not, but if we did not accept his suggestion then it looked as though we might have to take it the way it stood right then. He asked us to try living with the offered change for a while, and if it was unsatisfactory the matter could be brought up in the future.

Some of our people were not very happy. But this was now late in the summer of 1960 [just prior to the publication of the August revision] and it did look as though we might see it passed without getting even what was offered. Besides, we are a relatively small group, and I was worried that they might feel we were not worth too much trouble. So I called him up and told him we would accept his recommendation. He agreed and asked us to give our support at the September hearings, which we did.

The Fifth Avenue Association, a group high in prestige, with frequent contacts with the Planning Commission and other agencies of the city, and able to win space in the press for most of its activities, initially opposed the provisions for its area in the 1959 informal hearings. After consultation with the Planning Commission staff and members of the commission itself, it was allowed to "virtually write its own provisions." The Fifth Avenue Association was confident that its endorsement was needed and wanted, and that its demands could be high and would still be met.

At the base of these two cases are some of the major aspects of the bargaining process. The position of the group vis-à-vis other participants, the strength of its name or support, the timing of demands, and the ability to withstand pressure gave the Fifth Avenue Association an advantage in comparison with the first group. The homeowners' association was forced to confront the realization that a refusal to participate meant exclusion, while the Fifth Avenue Association, located in Manhattan and close to the processes of the system, did not fear exclusion.

The pattern in zoning has been that an unwillingness to bargain has meant to risk losing in the struggle. For the Planning Commission, failure to bargain in 1941 and again in 1949–52 resulted in defeat. In the struggle over the Moses plan the decision to make concessions came after the opposition had organized, and was thus too late. In 1960, for all the real estate boards except those of Staten Island and Manhattan, their exclusion from the bargaining process left them with little or no voice in the final product of the contest.

In its turn, however, the ability to bargain was related to the other complex features of the zoning system: interests, rules, position in the system, the operation of the other processes, and the commitments of the participants.

Summary

Although the zoning system was structured by the rules of the game and the interests of the participants, the general characteristics of the system and the processes modified the structure. The general characteristics served to surround the behavior of the actors with a "middle-class" style, thereby setting outer limits on the methods the participants could use in asserting their claims.

The strategic processes of the zoning system tended to modify the inherent localism of the system's structure. Prior to 1938, linkages among actors were vertical, between local groups and the governmental actors, with overt conflict dampened.

After 1938, the older pattern tended to break down, although the structure of the system (with its emphasis on localism) continued. To be effective, the participants turned to building temporary alliances to replace the set of accommodations used before 1938. In general, the groups opposing zoning amendments were more successful than the Planning Commission in the search for allies, in part because the Planning Commission until 1959–60 was reluctant to bargain with its proposals.

PART THREE

CONCLUSIONS

VII

THE POLITICS
OF ZONING

In New York City, the planner's vision to "knit together the
great variety of human activities into . . . a conceptualized
whole, a model, relating these activities to the physical environment" [1] through zoning, had an uncertain success. The efforts
to enact a rational and efficient model of the city consistently
foundered on the structure and processes of the zoning system.
Instead of the planner's model, the zoning system was an intri-
cate method for representing diverse claims against zoning as
public policy. Characteristically this system was marked by
moderate political behavior. There was a heavy emphasis on
bargaining as the vehicle through which local and specialized
participants were represented in the process. There was a multiplicity of participants—both governmental and nongovernmental—and these actors were committed to stakes in zoning that
often were noncongruent or in conflict and that, even more
often, were not in agreement with the goals of the planners and
the Reformers. These attributes of the politics of zoning carry
numerous implications for students of public policy, city planning, and urban systems. Without attempting to identify all
these implications, three are worth noting in detail. The first is
the role of the Reformers in zoning politics. The second is the
problem of innovation in a pluralistic system; the third, the
significance of zoning for our understanding of urban political
systems.

Reformers and the Public Interest

In New York City, the zoning system was by no means dominated by the Reformers. The New York municipal reform movement did, however, provide much of the initiative and motivating force behind efforts to achieve comprehensive zoning in the city.

City planning and zoning were not always or even most of the time the primary concerns of the Reformers. In their battles with the political "machines," their efforts to achieve Charter reform and "good government" in general, the Reformers usually allowed zoning to take a back seat. Nevertheless, the Citizens Union, the City Club, and, after 1930, the Regional Plan Association were the most frequent and active proponents of comprehensive zoning outside the City Planning Commission.

The Planning Commission was itself the reservoir of the Reformers' ideology in the city government. Although it often had difficulty maintaining its tenuous alliance with the Reform organizations, it nonetheless persistently advocated the "efficient, rational, and general" model of the city.

This model of the city—held in common by the Planning Commission and the Reform interest groups and also shared by the latecomer Reform Democrats—was based on a particular view of the "public interest." [2] The basic view held by the Reformers and city planners was a concept of the city as a "community." The community view argued that the city, as an entity, had an interest or a need beyond the simple collective needs of all the inhabitants, and that there was a way of expressing this interest in physical or procedural terms. In approaching the problems of the community, the planners-Reformers felt that "special interests" should be secondary or subordinate to the demands of the city-as-community. Although there was occasional disagreement as to how the interest of the community at large was best to be discovered,[3] there was no fundamental disagreement that the public interest did, in fact, exist and should come before any special interest.

Although most of the actors in the zoning system in New York explicitly or implicitly argued that their special interests were fundamental to the public interest, the planners and the Reformers tended to treat these claims as only propagandistic appeals (which many might well have been). The homeowners, realtors, and local businessmen, for example, argued that their special interests were so fundamental to the health of the city's economy or society that recognition of their claims was necessary for the public interest. The Reformers, on the other hand, generally took the position that the public interest in zoning was more than any mere summation of all private or special interests. And comprehensive zoning, with its complex interrelations of a wide range of social and physical factors, was one of the preferred ways to arrive at the public interest. Less-than-comprehensive zoning was a surrender to the private interests. The planners-Reformers did not take the unrealistic stance that there was no place for special or local interests in zoning, but they saw the problem as one of priorities. When the local groups claimed that their interests were essential to the public interest, the tendency of the planners was to ask: "Yes, but are they *sufficient?*"

In a political system that emphasized bargaining and concession, however, this relatively unbending view of the public interest placed a severe burden on the planners-Reformers. Tugwell and Orton, unable to negotiate, were also unable to win. The structure of the system—which gave localism and specialization a high degree of representation—and the processes that made this representation effective offered only two choices: accept defeat or undertake strategies of alliance building and concessions such as James Felt used.

Bassett, McAneny, and Felt were a different kind of planner-Reformer. Although they were strongly committed to zoning, their instinct, if not their conscious strategy, was to find a way of winning within the general context of comprehensive zoning. They were willing to bargain, and they were willing to sacrifice some aspects of the substantive content of the zoning proposals, although there was also a hard core beyond which they refused to go. This hard core was the concept of zoning in its comprehensive aspects. Bassett, McAneny, and Felt thus had a degree of flexibility: specific aspects of a proposal could be sacrificed to win victory.

The unanswered question remains, of course: How great can the sacrifices be and the proposal still be "comprehensive" in anything but name? Many of those around Felt believed that to win he went too far; in all probability Felt and many others would not agree. But the question raises a major dilemma for the Reformers as the guardians of the public interest: the demands of the system on the one hand and the demands of the planning-Reform ideology on the other.

The consequences of this dilemma were twofold for the politics of zoning. First, the Reformers played a basic role as the source of initiative and agitation for comprehensive zoning. They also provided the ideological raw materials for change. The Reformers were usually willing to accept innovation, to challenge the status quo. But, second, as any given struggle over zoning progressed, the Reformers' reluctance to bargain and to make concessions caused them to act as a negative force by threatening the chances of victory. James Felt was able to bargain, but he always had to keep one eye on the reactions of his staff and the supporting Reform interest groups. The zoning system had the capacity to produce innovation, but it could or would do so only when the commitments of the protagonists were amenable to the processes of the system.

Innovation and Zoning Politics

One of the most significant characteristics of zoning as public policy is that it is a conscious effort both to control change and

to produce change with the urban environment as its target.[4]
As we have seen, however, the zoning system in New York City
was highly resistant to change—both in policy content and in
the structure of the system. Changes did occur; the Planning
Commission came into being in 1938, and the 1960 Zoning
Resolution incorporated a number of innovations that had
been resisted at earlier times. Perhaps the major question is
then: How did these or any other changes in the system occur
- including the 1916 Resolution?

The answer would appear to lie in the structure and processes of the zoning system as it has already been described.
Basically, the zoning system was "pluralistic," that is, the zoning system in New York involved a large number of actors
whose interests were often in conflict or were at least noncongruent, and no single actor or set of actors was able totally
to dominate zoning policy-making. Typically, pluralistic systems are resistant to policy and structural changes. Bargaining,
however, is one of the major characteristics of pluralistic systems. Although bargaining requires concessions on the part of
the protagonists, it also permits resolution of conflicts and disagreements. This was the case for zoning in New York City.
And, for the zoning system in the city, bargaining was a major
process for producing change.

The actors' commitments to their interests—as long as these
commitments were to some degree flexible—were generally subject to bargaining. Through mutual concessions, and an unwillingness to go for "all or nothing," change in the structure
of the zoning system and change in the content of zoning policy
occurred. These changes usually fell short of the ideal of comprehensive zoning, but they represented a degree of innovation
that was tolerable to all or most of the participants. Bargaining,
moreover, perhaps provided the best means of accommodating
and representing the immensely diverse interests that zoning
touched.

In this sense, the other major processes—vertical and horizontal linkages, and accommodations through the political party organizations and the agencies of government—helped to serve the same purpose. These processes permitted and facilitated bargaining situations among mutually interested participants. The alternative, and this alternative was latent in the fragmented structure of the zoning system, was such unbending commitments and such complete lack of communication among the participants that no form of negotiation—and thereby no form of change—could occur.

Certainly a system for comprehensive zoning based on bargaining and concessions, and resting on more or less tenuous alliances, does not conform to the planners' and the Reformers' ideal of the best method to pursue the public interest. There are, however, advantages to a system structured in this fashion. Although the ideal of comprehensive zoning has never dominated zoning policy-making, neither has any one group or interest been able to prevail at all times. Few, if any, actors are systematically excluded from participation—in this sense the zoning system is relatively "open." Although advantages accrue to the knowledgeable and the skilled, although great emphasis is placed on a "middle-class" style in zoning politics, it can be argued that these characteristics help to ensure some degree of order and to provide a basis for communication. As has been noted of New York City's general political system, the system "may pay a cost in terms of engineering concepts of efficiency, but the system can justly claim to possess openness, responsiveness, and tolerance as essential characteristics of its democracy." [5]

And the record of zoning in New York City is not a dismal one. The first city to achieve modern comprehensive zoning in the United States, it has also been a forum and a laboratory for the testing of ideas and methods in zoning. It has placed great burdens on the advocates of zoning, but the potential capacity of these advocates to touch broad and signicant areas of the economic and social life of the city's inhabitants perhaps demands that they be willing to shoulder those burdens.

Zoning and Urban Political Systems

One of the major difficulties in studying one urban political system is the lack of firm assurance that any generalization based on that system applies to another city or town. Although urban areas doubtlessly have certain fundamental characteristics in common—ecological, economic, social, and political—at the present stage of research and analysis these characteristics still defy easy classification and are often the topics of scholarly disagreements. Further, the relationships among the fundamental characteristics are even less easy to describe. For example, would parallels between two cities in economic terms necessarily imply parallels in political systems? And, what are the politically relevant economic, social, or demographic variables?

Nor do the problems stop here. We have already seen the importance of the structure of the political system to the processes of the system. Do differences in structure always lead to differences in process? New York City is unique in its major legislative institution, the Board of Estimate. In other cities, where there is no comparable institution, would the zoning system operate in a similar or different manner? In another city, where the homeowners, for example, have not achieved the high degree of organization that they have in New York City, would organizations appear under the impetus of a zoning proposal? Could they bargain so effectively?

The answers to these questions, and to the many other questions that arise in the course of a study of urban policy-making, must await further research. For the sake of future explorations, however, it is worth the effort to attempt to plot some possible alternatives, drawing where possible on research that has already been conducted.

Initially we justified an examination of the politics of zoning because it might well provide an effective window to the politics of New York City. This justification was based on the logic that comprehensive zoning involved a wide array of governmental, economic, social, and ideological interests. At the risk of overstating the case, zoning proposals required these interests to interact, to seek points of contact, and to settle conflicts of goals and aspirations.[6]

The processes of settlement in zoning politics bear a close resemblance to the general nature of politics and government in New York City as described by Sayre and Kaufman. In broad terms, Sayre and Kaufman saw New York City politics moving in two main directions: an increased role for the city's bureaucracy [7] and a degree of centralization despite the continuance of the fundamentally pluralistic nature of the system.[8] Centralization, as these authors see it, tends to occur around specific policy areas or specific governmental agencies in a cluster effect.[9] Negotiation, bargaining, and settlement of competing claims tend to occur within these clusters. Further, there is a constant tendency to favor the status quo, although innovation can and does happen.[10]

Zoning politics in New York City conforms to this more generalized description. There are variations; the role of the Reformers was perhaps more significant in zoning than in the politics of education, law enforcement, or traffic planning, for example. But the main point still holds: in general, the politics of zoning in New York City presents a fair description of the politics of the city as a whole.[11]

Whether this would, in fact, be true of other cities is less easy to answer. On the one hand, there are few generally descriptive works of the politics of other cities readily available, and there are even fewer studies of the politics of zoning. It may be argued, however, that the politics of comprehensive zoning in other cities would tend to reflect the general outline of the politics of the given city. In a city in which the business-men dominated the political system, in all probability they would also dominate in zoning policy-making.[12] In a city where the economic interests were forced to compete with organized social interests in other policy areas, this competition should be reflected in zoning politics.

As a policy area, zoning in New York City has certain strik-ing characteristics. Williams and Adrian[13] have postulated four model types for the political process. These types—the promo-tion of economic growth, the provision of life's amenities, the maintenance of traditional services, and arbitration among conflicting interests—represent four differing approaches to-ward the role of government and governmental policy. As Wil-liams and Adrian point out, these types will appear as an ad-mixture within any given city. In fact, in New York City, it appears that at least three of the four types play important roles in the politics of zoning. To a great extent, the economic interests focus on zoning as a means of promoting economic growth; the homeowners, and to some extent the Reformers, turned to zoning for the provision of life's amenities; and all the participants relied on the processes of the zoning system to arbitrate conflicts. Of the four categories, the maintenance of traditional services appears to have played the least prominent part.

This would suggest that New York City, in its vast complex-ity, encompasses the roles of government that Williams and Adrian hypothesize. An addition would perhaps even be re-quired: the role of the Reformers suggests that a perceived task of government and governmental policy is to rationalize and control the urban environment. It also suggests that zon-ing is a sufficiently broad and immediate policy area as to evoke the spectrum of responses to government and governmental activity. In a city that is less diversified and specialized than New York, one of these types might tend to be the dominating one—and zoning itself might well be a means for expressing these values.[14] That is, viewed on a cultural dimension, zoning may be reflective of various cultural orientations, and may be a means of understanding how these cultural perspectives are articulated through the political system. In a small suburban community, for example, where property values, spacious lots, comfortable houses, and the absence of commercial uses are the desired goals of the "neighborhood virtues," zoning laws might be written and supported to reflect these values (life's amenities).[15] An examination of a number of communities and a comparison on a percentage basis of the land areas given over to particular uses might help to verify this hypothesis if coupled with a more general survey of the political processes of the communities.

As public policy, zoning has an important geographic or areal dimension. The homeowners, real estate groups, local business groups, and local civic associations construed their interests in terms of their "jurisdictions"—the geographic areas that constituted the base for their constituencies. This geographic dimension played a significant part in shaping the structure of the zoning system, and it strongly affected the system's processes. It was difficult for groups with different areal bases to form alliances; the Planning Commission, for one, was forced to deal with groups from different areas in terms of their jurisdictions, even though these groups might fall into the same category of "functional" interests (that is, economic or social).

Other urban policy areas have similar geographic dimensions, education policy, law enforcement, and urban renewal, for example. The extent to which these policy areas have an areal base may affect both the structure of the political system and the processes that occur. Kaplan, for one, in studying urban renewal[16] concluded that the urban renewal system in Newark was closer to being "integrated" than it was to being "open-ended." In an integrated system, there is less overt conflict, more innovation, and a tighter control by a smaller number of participants. In an "open-ended" system (and zoning politics in New York City would conform to this description) there is "overt conflict . . . occurring among a wide variety of affected interests." [17] Outcomes are difficult to predict, it is relatively easy for actors to gain entrance to the system, and bargaining and compromise are more generalized than in an integrated system.

One possible explanation for this difference among systems may well lie in the fact that an urban renewal project affects only limited areas of a city at one time. Those outside the area are apt to have only limited interest in the project or its possible effects. Although there may be sharp controversy within the affected area,[18] the number and range of the participants, and the scope of the conflict, are limited. It is, moreover, likely that the interest groups involved regard the entire area as their jurisdiction. Interests may be in conflict, but interest groups are not unaware of or indifferent to each other. The possibilities of building alliances encompassing the whole area of conflict are increased. It may be easier for one group or set of interests to achieve a position of dominance.[19]

There are other factors, however, which should not be overlooked. The general political system may be sufficiently integrated as to dampen or overcome localized concerns successfully. This appears to have been the case in New Haven [20] in both urban renewal and education, although the leadership in both cases felt compelled to take local urges into account in making its decisions.[21]

It appears that the areal dimension in urban policy-making is sufficiently important to warrant further systematic study. Geographic delimitation in the "jurisdictions" of interests, both governmental (as in the case of the borough presidents) and nongovernmental, appears to be a pervasive and crucial factor in zoning politics. It may well be so in other policy areas. The areal dimension can affect the pattern of bargaining, the nature and extent of alliances, the kinds of concessions, and thereby the final outcome of the policy-making process.[22]

Zoning and the Future

Whether zoning can ever be a completely effective method of controlling the urban environment lies outside the scope of this study. Zoning may or may not be the best way to discover and implement the public interest, but it is clear that zoning will continue to be an important weapon in the city planner's arsenal. Urban renewal is presently the most publicized tool for attacking urban problems, but disillusionment has begun to set in,[23] and urban renewal to some extent must take place within the envelope of the more comprehensive methods of zoning and master planning.

The technology of zoning is constantly undergoing refinement. New methods of analyzing existing conditions, of making future projections, and of translating these into workable policy statements and proposals are increasingly objects of debate and discussion within city planning circles. At the same time, structural changes are being made in the forms of city governments to assist the planners in applying their techniques.[24] But it would seem safe to say that the success of the technical refinements will depend not only upon their intrinsic merits but also upon the political nature of the zoning systems in which they are advocated.

The formal governmental changes are, of course, another matter. Some changes—those which propose to strengthen planning agencies by placing them directly under the formal authority of the chief executive of the city[25]—may have a widespread impact on the success of zoning proposals. Such arrangements may have the effect of giving the mayor or city manager a stronger commitment to proposals originating in the planning agency. It also seems possible, however, that, without substantial changes in the calculus of risks surrounding the office of the chief executive, the basic structure of zoning may change very little. The politics and administration of zoning are rooted not only in the formal rules of the game but in the entire structure and processes of the political system.

The real and often final test of a zoning proposal is whether it can survive in the political arena. The real and final test of the ideals and goals of the proponents of city planning and municipal reform may be whether they can learn to cope with the demands the political environment makes upon their ideology.

APPENDIX A

POPULATION OF NEW YORK CITY BY COUNTY, 1900–1960

County	1900	1910	1920	1930	1940	1950	1960
New York	1,850,093	2,331,542	2,284,103	1,867,312	1,889,924	1,960,101	1,698,281
Kings	1,666,582	1,634,351	2,018,356	2,560,401	2,698,285	2,738,175	2,627,319
Bronx	200,507	430,980	732,016	1,265,258	1,394,111	1,451,277	1,424,815
Queens	152,999	284,041	469,042	1,079,129	1,297,634	1,550,849	1,809,578
Richmond	67,021	85,969	116,531	158,346	174,441	191,555	221,991
New York City	3,937,202	4,766,883	5,620,048	6,930,446	7,454,395	7,891,957	7,781,984

Source: U.S. Census, *Number of Inhabitants, New York State* (Washington, D.C., 1960).

APPENDIX B

DENSITY OF POPULATION IN NEW YORK CITY
BY BOROUGH, 1910–1960

Borough	Land area (square miles)	NUMBER OF PERSONS PER SQUARE MILE IN THOUSANDS					
		1910	1920	1930	1940	1950	1960
Manhattan	22	106	104	85	86	89	77
Brookyn	76	22	27	34	36	36	35
Bronx	43	10	16	29	32	34	33
Queens	113	3	4	9	11	14	16
Staten Island	60	1	2	3	3	3	4
New York City	314	15	18	22	24	25	25

Source: Computed from U.S. Census, *Number of Inhabitants, New York State* (Washington, D.C., 1960).

NOTES

Introduction

1. According to the International City Manager's Association, of the 1,021 cities with populations over 10,000 reporting to the association in 1960, 979 had zoning ordinances in effect. Of the 98 cities of populations of 100,000 or over, only three had no zoning. Orin F. Nolting and David S. Arnold, eds., *Municipal Year Book: 1960* (Chicago, International City Manager's Association, 1960), pp. 280–81.

2. There are any number of zoning legal textbooks that are representative of this approach. See, e.g., E. C. Yokley, *Zoning Law and Practice* (Charlottesville, Michie Company, 1953).

3. See, e.g., Robert M. Leary, *A Model Procedure for the Administration of Zoning Regulations* (Washington, D.C., Urban Land Institute, 1958).

4. For a more sophisticated definition of a "system" see Morton A. Kaplan, *System and Process in International Politics* (New York, John Wiley and Sons, 1957), p. 4, where a system is described as "a set of variables so related . . . that describable behavioral regularities characterize the internal relationships of the variables to each other."

Chapter I: The Resolution of 1916

1. In New York City, the five boroughs and five counties are coterminous. The five boroughs, with the county names in parentheses, are: Manhattan (New York); Brooklyn (Kings); the Bronx (Bronx); Queens (Queens); and Staten Island (Richmond). At the time of consolidation, Manhattan (plus parts of the Bronx) and Brooklyn were two separate cities.

2. Wallace S. Sayre and Herbert Kaufman, *Governing New York City: Politics in the Metropolis* (New York, Russell Sage Foundation, 1960), pp. 11–17, describe the struggle for control of the new city.

3. To complicate matters further, votes on the board were weighted, i.e., the three "city-wide" officers had three votes each, the presidents of Manhattan and Brooklyn two each, and the remaining borough presidents one each, for a total of sixteen. It would thus seem that the city-wide officers could easily control the board, but in fact they were often in conflict with each other. *Ibid.,* p. 16.

4. Michael D. Gilbert, "The Life and Work of a Municipal Interest Group: The Citizens Union of New York" (Columbia University doctoral dissertation in preparation), Chapters 1 and 2.

5. *Ibid.* Richard Hofstadter, *The Age of Reform: From Bryan to F.D.R.* (New York, Alfred A. Knopf, 1955), p. 183, says the Reformer's abstractions were "citizenship, responsibility, good government, economy, business-like management." See also Citizens Union, "Declaration of Principles and Objects," February 22, 1897.

6. Edward C. Banfield and James Q. Wilson, *City Politics* (Cambridge, Mass., Harvard University Press and M.I.T. Press, 1963), p. 139, comment: "The Reformers assumed that there existed an interest (the 'public interest') that pertained to the city 'as a whole' and that should always prevail over competing partial (and usually private) interests."

7. Until 1905 the mayor held office for only two years. The Fusion mayor elected in 1901 was Seth Low. The Regular Democratic mayor elected in 1903 and 1905 was George B. McClellan, Jr. Sources for the city's politics for the period 1898 to 1917 are: Sayre and Kaufman, *Governing New York City,* pp. 688–89, 694–95; Charles Garrett, *The La Guardia Years: Machine and Reform Politics in New York City* (New Brunswick, Rutgers University Press, 1961), pp. 10–14; Theodore Lowi, *At the Pleasure of the Mayor: Patronage and Power in New York City, 1898–1958* (New York, Free Press of Glencoe, 1964), especially Chapter 8.

8. The major source on George McAneny is his own "Reminiscences," contained in the Columbia University Oral History Collection.

9. The principal source for the characterization of Edward M. Bassett is an interview with his son, Howard M. Bassett (January 8, 1963). Mr. Bassett has the complete newspaper scrapbook of his father, which is a full file of the life of Edward Bassett and was

generously used for this study. See also Edward M. Bassett, *Auto-biography* (New York, Harbor Press, 1939).

10. The population density of the city was increasing. In 1900 there were 10,000 persons per square mile for the city as a whole. In 1910 the density was 15,000 per square mile.

11. The Reformers felt strongly about overcrowding. Bassett— "the Father of City Planning"—opposed public housing in the 1930s because it increased density. Bassett, *Autobiography*, p. 134, where he also commented: "My interest in zoning was largely based on sunlight." McAneny in his "Reminiscences" said (p. 34): "[High buildings] robbed their neighbors of light and air and filled the streets with the density of the moving population."

12. Edwin H. Spengler, "Land Values in New York in Relation to Transit Facilities" (Columbia University doctoral dissertation, 1930), traces in detail the real estate slump of 1907–15. See also W. J. Ulmer, "Zoning from the Viewpoint of the Lender on Real Estate Mortgages," in National Conference on City Planning, *Proceedings of the Twelfth Annual Conference* (Cincinnati, 1920).

13. New York City Charter (1901), Section 43.

14. These cases were resolved as follows: for Los Angeles, in *Hadacheck* v. *Sebastian*, 36 S. Ct. 143 (1915); for Boston, in *Welch* v. *Swasey*, 29 S. Ct. 567 (1909). The latter case, which was resolved in time to be of use to Bassett and McAneny, involved issues that were not much more extensive than the powers granted the Board of Aldermen under tenement house control.

15. Testimony of Bruce Falconer to the Heights of Buildings Commission, *Report* of the Commission, December, 1913, pp. 52–53.

16. Lawson Purdy, "Reminiscences," Columbia University Oral History Collection, p. 26.

17. Fifth Avenue Association, *Annual Report*, 1907.

18. *Ibid.*, 1911.

19. *Report of the Fifth Avenue Commission to the President of the Borough of Manhattan*, 1912.

20. McAneny and Bassett were conferring on a regular basis at this time. In the light of subsequent events, it seems probable that the two discussed the legal and political difficulties of the Fifth Avenue Commission proposal. Bassett, *Autobiography*, p. 119 and *passim*.

21. Board of Estimate and Apportionment, *Minutes*, meeting of May 9, 1912 (hereafter cited as Board Minutes).

22. Fifth Avenue Association, *Annual Report*, 1912.

23. McAneny, "Reminiscences," p. 35.

24. Board Minutes, February 27, 1913.

25. *Ibid.*

26. *Ibid.*

27. *Ibid.*

28. They were Brooklyn Borough President Lewis H. Pounds and Bronx Borough President Cyrus C. Miller.

29. McAneny, "Reminiscences," p. 16 and *passim;* Purdy, "Reminiscences," pp. 25–26.

30. H. M. Bassett interview.

31. The members of the commission were, with their principal occupation and borough indicated in parentheses: E. M. Bassett (lawyer, Brooklyn); E. C. Blum (merchant, Brooklyn); E. M. Brown (manufacturer, Staten Island); W. H. Chesebrough (realtor, Manhattan; W. A. Cokeley (realtor, Bronx); O. M. Eideltz (builder, Manhattan); A. I. Elkus (lawyer, Manhattan); B. L. Fenner (architect, Manhattan); J. M. Hewlett (architect, Brooklyn); R. G. Higbie (manufacturer, Queens); C. G. LaFarge (architect, Manhattan); G. T. Mortimer (realtor, Brooklyn); A. Robinson (realtor, Manhattan); A. F. Schwarzler (builder, Bronx); F. S. Tomlin (labor leader, Brooklyn); Lawrence Veiller (tenement house commissioner and tenement house reformer, Manhattan); G. S. White (minister and professor of theology, Manhattan). Sources: *Who's Who in New York,* 1914, 1918. The remaining two, Nelson P. Lewis (chief engineer of the Board of Estimate) and Lawson Purdy (city tax assessor), were representing the city's interests.

Thus, there were four realtors; two lawyers; two manufacturers; two builders; one professional labor leader; one merchant; three architects; two members of the city government; a Presbyterian minister; and a tenement house reformer.

32. Purdy, "Reminiscences," p. 28.

33. New York *Times,* March 23, April 13, 1913.

34. *Ibid.,* April 20, 1913.

35. Fifth Avenue Association, *Annual Report,* 1913.

36. Testimony submitted to the Heights of Buildings Commission, contained in the commission's *Report,* December, 1913 (hereafter cited as First Commission Report).

37. *Ibid.*

38. *Ibid.*

39. New York *Times,* June 13, 1913.

40. *Ibid.,* July 3, 1913.

41. *Ibid.,* July 13, 1913. Bassett was, publicly at least, still uncertain how to approach the legal problem. He was worried about "discrimination" against the factories on Fifth Avenue, although

in an interview with the New York *Times,* June 29, 1913, he mentioned that the "health and safety" provisions of the police power "might be" legal grounds for regulation.

42. Purdy, "Reminiscences," p. 29.

43. *Ibid.,* p. 31.

44. Reprinted in First Commission Report.

45. New York *Times,* December 5, 1913.

46. First Commission Report, p. 3.

47. *Ibid.*

48. *Ibid.*

49. Purdy, "Reminiscences," p. 31.

50. Specifically, the Board of Estimate was empowered to pass laws to "regulate the height and bulk of buildings hereafter erected" and to "regulate and restrict the location of trades and industries and the location of buildings designed for specified uses, and may divide the city into districts . . . to carry out the purpose of this section." Chapter 470, New York State Laws of 1914, Section 242.

51. Purdy, "Reminiscences," pp. 23–24; Edna Amberg and William H. Allen, *Civic Lessions from Mayor Mitchel's Defeat* (New York, Institute for Public Service, 1921); Edwin R. Lewinson, "John Purroy Mitchel: Symbol of Reform" (Columbia University doctoral dissertation, 1961).

52. E. M. Bassett, Speech to the Chicago Real Estate Board, November 13, 1922, reprinted in *Studies on Building Height Limitations in Large Cities* (Chicago, Chicago Real Estate Board, 1923). Quotations used by permission.

53. First Commission Report, Appendix A.

54. McAneny, "Reminiscences," p. 16.

55. New York *Times,* May 17, 1914.

56. Board Minutes, May 19, 1914.

57. *Ibid.,* May 22, 1914.

58. For the text of the resolution, see the Commission on Building Districts and Restrictions, *Report,* June 2, 1914 (hereafter cited as Second Commission Report).

59. Board Minutes, May 22, 1914.

60. Members of the Second Commission, with their principle occupation and borough indicated in parentheses, were: E. M. Bassett (lawyer, Brooklyn, also on First Commission); E. C. Blum (merchant, Brooklyn, also on First Commission); J. E. Clonin (labor leader, Manhattan); O. M. Eidletz (builder, Manhattan, also on First Commission); E. R. Hardy (insurance executive, Manhattan); R. W. Lawrence (manufacturer, Bronx); A. H. Man (lawyer, Queens); A. E. Marling (realtor, Manhattan); G. T. Mortimer (real-

tor, Brooklyn, also on First Commission); J. F. Smith (retail merchant, Brooklyn); Walter Stabler (finance executive, Manhattan); F. S. Tomlin (labor leader, Brooklyn, also on First Commission); G. C. Whipple (civil engineer, Manhattan); W. C. Willcox (insurance executive, Staten Island); Lawson Purdy (city government, also on First Commission). Sources: *Who's Who in New York,* 1914, 1918.

61. Borough representation was: Manhattan, seven; Brooklyn, five; the Bronx, one; Queens, one; Staten Island, one. The number of architects declined from three to one. The "world of finance" had a heavier representation on the Second Commission, and labor had increased its representation by one.

62. Bassett, Speech.

63. *Ibid.*

64. Gordon B. Ford, "How New York City Now Controls the Development of Private Property" (1916?), pamphlet on file at Columbia University Avery Library.

65. H. M. Bassett interview.

66. Purdy, "Reminiscences," p. 28.

67. Board of Estimate and Appointment, Committee on City Planning, *Transcript of the Public Hearings,* January, 1915.

68. *Ibid.* Allan Robinson was spokesman for this group. Robinson had served on the First Zoning Commission and was an active member of the Fifth Avenue Association.

69. *Ibid.*

70. New York *Times,* December 15, 1915.

71. *Ibid.,* December 16, 1915.

72. *Ibid.,* April 28, 1915.

73. *Ibid.,* January 16, 1916. See also Fifth Avenue Association, *Annual Report,* 1916.

74. New York *Times,* January 26, 1916.

75. *Ibid.,* January 27, 1916.

76. *Ibid.,* January 30, 1916.

77. Specifically, the Title Guarantee and Trust Company and the Lawyers Trust and Guaranty Company. *Ibid.,* February 4, 1916.

78. *Ibid.,* February 6, 1916.

79. McAneny resigned from the presidency of the Board of Aldermen for financial reasons, February 1, 1916. He became the executive manager of the New York *Times* until 1921, then chairman of the New York State Transit Commission for five years. In 1930 he became president of the Regional Plan Association (which he had helped to found). His resignation from the Board of Aldermen did not prevent his continuing to fight for zoning, and there is no

doubt that his opinions were listened to both within the city government and outside it.

80. New York *Times,* March 1, 1916.

81. See, e.g., the New York *Times,* March 5, 1916.

82. *Ibid.*

83. *Ibid.* The western boundary of the "deadlined" zone was Seventh Avenue; the eastern, Third Avenue.

84. *Ibid.*

85. *Ibid.,* March 9, 1916.

86. *Ibid.*

87. The Second Commission Report carries a reprint of the resolution. The phrasing of the financial institutions' resolution suggests that they turned to members of the commission for at least aid in drafting the document.

88. New York *Times,* March 23, 1916. The purpose of the Broadway Commission was to preserve the hotel district by prohibiting factories from the midtown Broadway area.

89. *Ibid.,* March 26, 28, 1916. Fifth Avenue Association, *Annual Report,* 1916. The Central Fifth Avenue Committee seems to have been inspired by the Fifth Avenue Association, and, on March 27, the association voted to extend its own "deadline" to Twenty-second Street.

90. Although transcripts were taken of the hearings, apparently not all the transcripts are extant. Partial transcripts were uncovered for the hearings of March 27 and 29, April 17 and 18, and what appears to be a complete transcript for March 28. The comments in the text have been pieced together from these transcripts and reports of the hearings in the New York *Times* and the New York *Sun.*

91. Some of these groups were: the West Side Taxpayers Association, the Greater New York Taxpayers Association (both chiefly real estate organizations), the Washington Square Association, the Park Avenue Association, and the newly formed Murray Hill Association, which was dominated by J. P. Morgan.

92. New York *Times,* April 2, 1916.

93. Quoted *ibid.,* April 3, 1916.

94. *Ibid.,* May 30, 1916.

95. *Ibid.*

96. Board Minutes, June 2, 1916.

97. Second Commission Report.

98. *Ibid.*

99. *Ibid.*

100. The Board of Standards and Appeals had been established

on April 17, 1916, by amendment to the Charter, New York City Charter (1901), Section 242a. New York *Times,* April 18, 1916.

101. The Fifth Avenue area was put into the two most restrictive bulk categories, but the other areas of downtown Manhattan had only very limited restrictions imposed upon them.

102. New York *Times,* June 16, 1916.

103. Board of Estimate and Apportionment, Subcommittee on the Relation of the Proposed Plan to Other Plans of City Development, *Report,* June 15, 1916.

104. *Ibid.* Board of Estimate and Apportionment, Subcommittee to Consider the Districting Resolution, *Report,* June 15, 1916.

105. Board Minutes, June 19, 21, 27, and 29, 1916.

106. Board of Estimate and Apportionment, Committee on City Planning, *Report,* July 18, 1916.

107. Board Minutes, July 25, 1916.

Chapter II: The Years of Frustration, 1917–1945

1. At the same time (during the 1920s and 1930s) Bassett carried the experience he had gained in New York City to the rest of the country, advocating zoning in nearly all the states of the nation. Although not universally successful—both New Jersey and Pennsylvania, for example, were slow to approve zoning—zoning rapidly became a popular method for attacking urban problems in the post World War I era. See Robert Walker, *The Planning Function in Urban Government* (Chicago, University of Chicago Press, 1950), pp. 27–32. Walker points out that by 1936, just twenty years after the passage of the 1916 Resolution, 1,322 cities had zoning ordinances (p. 32).

2. Sources for the city's politics, 1917 to 1945, are Charles Garrett, *The La Guardia Years: Machine and Reform Politics in New York City* (New Brunswick, Rutgers University Press, 1961), and Warren Moscow, *Politics in the Empire State* (New York, Alfred A. Knopf, 1948).

3. A close reading of the *New York Times Index* for the period 1917 to 1937 reveals both the number and the kinds of requests made to the Board of Estimate.

4. New York *Times,* August 18, 1923; March 28, 1926; July 12, 1927; May 18, 1928; December 6, 1930; July 21, 1935.

5. Most notably, the famous "Murray Hill Fight" (1916 to 1935). *Ibid.,* February 24, 1918; March 4, 1923; April 7, 1936. Other examples of strategic delays: *ibid.,* December 10, 1921; April 20, 1926.

6. See also John P. Comer, *New York City Building Control, 1800–1941* (New York, Columbia University Press, 1942), pp. 116, 138–39, 153–54.

7. *Ibid.,* pp. 199–200, and p. 201 where Comer comments: "Chairman Walsh's [of the BSA] chief fitness lay in his . . . close personal and political friendship with Mayor Hylan and the more powerful Tammany leaders, and in his seeing eye to eye with such leaders."

8. New York *Times,* February 5, March 25, 1924.

9. Mayor's Committee on City Planning and Survey, *Report,* 1928.

10. *Ibid.*

11. New York *Times,* October 3, 1926; February 27, 1927.

12. See, e.g., the American Academy of Political and Social Science, *Annals,* Vol. 155, Part II (May, 1931): *Zoning in the United States.*

13. One critic of the committee said: "Many of these committee members had little previous knowledge of the subject committed to them and had even less time or inclination to study them." Fine Arts Federation of New York City, "Review of City Development," pp. 3–4 (1938).

14. Mayor's Committee on City Planning, *Report.*

15. New York *Times,* April 12, May 30, August 7, August 26, 1928.

16. *Ibid.,* especially August 26, 1928.

17. *Ibid.,* November 14, 1928.

18. *Ibid.,* February 27, 1929. McAneny also offered a proposal for a planning body that would have from five to seven members, and requiring a three-quarters veto on the Board of Estimate to overrule action by the planning body. *Ibid.,* November 16, 1928.

19. The commission was to be composed of the chief engineer of the Board of Estimate and two mayoral appointees. *Ibid.,* February 27, 1929.

20. New York State, *Legislative Record and Index,* 1929.

21. New York *Times,* March 12, 1929.

22. *Ibid.*

23. *Ibid.,* March 23, 1929.

24. *Ibid.,* March 27, 1929.

25. *Ibid.,* March 28, March 29, 1929.

26. *Ibid.,* March 30, 1929.

27. Board of Estimate and Apportionment, Minutes, May 23, 1930. The proposed planning department was charged with keeping

the official map of the city up to date and making a scale model of the city.

28. New York *Times,* May 24, 1930.

29. *Ibid.,* June 7, 1930.

30. Board Minutes, June 25, 1930. In the hearing preceding the vote, Flynn said he would vote for the proposal if the planning body had no powers already granted to the chief engineer of the Board of Estimate. The Citizens Union opposed the proposal, but the City Club and a number of local business and real estate groups favored it. New York *Times,* June 26, 1930.

31. Walker's proposal passed the Board of Aldermen with ease in July, 1930. The vote was fifty-seven to one. The lone dissenter, a Democrat from Brooklyn, argued that the bill was a threat to borough autonomy. New York *Times,* July 8 and 9, 1930.

32. By this time the mayor was J. P. O'Brien, who succeeded Walker in 1933 when the latter was forced to resign as a result of the scandals uncovered by the Seabury investigations.

33. Cleveland Rodgers, "Reminiscences," Columbia University Oral History Collection, pp. 149–50.

34. New York *Times,* November 28,1933; March 2, 1934.

35. *Ibid.,* February 8, 1935.

36. The members of the Charter Commission were: Thomas D. Thacher; J. D. McGoldrick, lawyer, Columbia University instructor, and active La Guardia supporter; Judge F. L. Hackenburg; Judge J. M. Proskauer; T. I. Parkinson; C. G. Garrison; S. J. Block; and Mrs. Genevieve Earl, executive secretary of the Womens City Club. New York *Times,* April 27, 1936.

37. A typical statement of the issues appears in the New York *Times,* March 10, 1935.

38. Citizens Union memorandum to the New York City Charter Revision Commission, dated January 29, 1935, in New York City Charter Revision Commission, *Records,* Vol. II (hereafter cited as Charter Commission).

39. Statement of Raymond Ingersoll to Charter Commission, March 12, 1935.

40. Statement of Vernon Moon, chief engineer of the Board of Estimate, to Charter Commission, March 19, 1935.

41. Statement of George U. Harvey, Queens borough president, to Charter Commission, April 15, 1935.

42. Statement of James Lyons to Charter Commission, April 17, 1935.

43. Statement of J. A. Palma to Charter Commission, April 23, 1935.

44. *Ibid.*

45. Statement of F. La Guardia to Charter Commission, May 9, 1935.

46. Statement of E. M. Bassett to Charter Commission, May 16, 1935.

47. Charter Commission Minutes, May 16, 1935.

48. Charter Commission memorandum, June 3, 1935 (unsigned), clearly implies that the commission was worried by the opposition of the borough presidents.

49. Charter Commission Minutes, June 4, 1935.

50. *Ibid.*

51. Not all of the Charter Commission members were equally committed to the idea of a planning commission. Proskauer and Meyer (who had served on quasi-official planning agencies in Queens), McGoldrick, and members of the staff all favored a central planning agency. Thacher, however, was more concerned with the complex fiscal and intrapolitical problems of the city's government. Rodgers, "Reminiscences," p. 197.

52. Chapter Commission memorandum, July 18, 1935.

53. See the letter from the Queens Citizens Committee for Borough Autonomy (June 22, 1935) to Charter Commission, contained in the minutes of that date.

54. The data show that, in spite of efforts to stimulate interest in the planning commission concept, there were very few who responded.

55. Charter Commission Minutes, October 1, 1935.

56. *Ibid.,* October 22, 1935. It is not clear who offered this solution.

57. *Ibid.*

58. *Ibid.*

59. *Ibid.,* October 24, 1935.

60. The authorship of the report is in doubt. Joseph D. McGoldrick, in a letter to the author (May 28, 1963), said, "Among the members, mine was the principal hand." He went on to say, "I had less to do with provisions re . . . zoning, etc. Lawrence Tanzer, associate counsel to the Charter Commission, may have written these."

61. Charter Commission, Report on "City Planning," April 8, 1935.

62. Charter Commission, *Preliminary Report,* April, 1936, pp. 9–11.

63. The hearings were held in Brooklyn on May 11, 1936; the Bronx, on May 14; Manhattan, on May 19; Queens, on May 21; Staten Island, on May 22; and Manhattan again, on May 26, 1936.

64. Lyons, for example, said that the Planning Commission "is

one of the most dangerous weapons for the destruction of home rule and local government." Charter Commission Public Hearings (hereafter cited as Charter Hearings), Bronx Hearings, May 14, 1936.

65. The Staten Island borough president admitted that he thought Staten Island had an "inferiority complex" and was thus suspicious of any proposal. Charter Hearings, Staten Island, May 22, 1936.

66. See, e.g., New York *Times,* April 27, 1936.

67. *Ibid.,* June 1, 6, 14; July 3; August 19, 21; September 17, 20, 23, 30; October 2, 28, 29, 30; November 2, 3, 4, 1936.

68. During July, Lyons made an effort to forestall a Planning Commission in the Charter by action by the Board of Estimate. He proposed a resolution to establish a City Board composed of the borough engineers and with only advisory functions. Ingersoll, the mayor, and the comptroller voted against the Lyons proposal; the president of the Board of Aldermen abstained, and the motion failed. New York *Times,* July 16, 1936.

69. Board of Elections, *Annual Report,* 1936. Staten Island was the only borough to vote against the proposed charter.

70. McGoldwick, in his letter to the author (May 28, 1963), recalled that he could not remember any opposition to the idea of a City Planning Commission from nongovernmental interest groups.

71. This analysis closely follows Wallace S. Sayre and Herbert Kaufman, *Governing New York City: Politics in the Metropolis* (New York, Russell Sage Foundation, 1960), pp. 372–73.

72. Cleveland Rodgers, "Reminiscences," p. 200, said, "The first members of the Commission, I am convinced, were named by Mayor La Guardia without political consideration." Rexford G. Tugwell, in an interview (July 15, 1963), did not share this view. Tugwell was convinced that Sheridan was appointed to represent Bronx Borough President Lyons on the commission. There is no evidence that the mayor attempted to achieve borough representation, however.

73. Rodgers believed that the commission should work in an advisory and project-by-project basis; Sheridan favored deference to borough interests; Salmon apparently shared some of these views. Rodgers, *ibid.,* pp. 200–201.

74. *Ibid.,* p. 189.

75. New York *Times,* December 2, 1937. Lawrence Orton, at the time of his appointment to the Planning Commission, was by far the most city planning oriented member of the commission. From the time of his graduation from Cornell University in 1923 he had

worked almost without break with the Regional Plan Association in various capacities. *Who's Who in New York,* 1938.

76. New York *Times,* January 10, 1938.

77. Sources on Tugwell are numerous. For Tugwell's views on city planning, see Rexford G. Tugwell, "Implementing the General Interest," *Public Administration Review,* Vol. I (Autumn, 1940); Rexford G. Tugwell, "The Fourth Power," *Planning and Civic Comment,* Vol. V (April-June, 1939).

78. Rodgers, "Reminiscences," p. 193.

79. See Tugwell, "Implementing the General Interest."

80. The New York *Times,* August 19, 1938, gives a full account of this struggle. See also City Planning Commission, *Annual Report,* 1938; New York *Times,* September 23, 1938.

81. City Planning Commission, *Minutes,* meeting of May 3, 1939 (hereafter cited as CPC Minutes). The two new use districts were an intermediate district between "unrestricted" and "business" districts and a more restrictive "residential" district.

82. *Ibid.,* May 24, 1939.

83. *Ibid.,* June 1 and 5, 1939.

84. *Ibid.,* June 14, 1939.

85. Tugwell, "Implementing the General Interest."

86. CPC Minutes, June 28, 1939.

87. *Ibid.,* June 30, 1939.

88. *Ibid.*

89. New York *Times,* November 16, 1939.

90. *Ibid.,* November 19, 1939.

91. CPC Minutes, November 22, 1939.

92. New York *Times,* November 26, 1939.

93. *Ibid.*

94. The Planning Commission probably did not seek help from the mayor, either. La Guardia had little sympathy with long-range planning and had very little interest in the Planning Commission. Rodgers, "Reminiscences," p. 237.

95. New York *Times,* February 1, 1940.

96. City Planning Commission, *Annual Report,* 1939.

97. *Ibid.*

98. New York *Times,* March 30, 1940.

99. CPC Minutes, May 29, 1940.

100. Among the groups filing objections were the Merchants Association, the New York Chamber of Commerce, the New York (Manhattan) Board of Trade, and the five borough real estate boards.

101. New York *Times,* June 16, 1940.

102. *Ibid.,* June 19, 1940.

103. The account of the meeting was drawn from the New York *Times,* June 21, 1940, and from the Board of Estimate, *Journal of Proceedings* (hereafter cited as Estimate Proceedings), meeting of June 20, 1940.

104. New York *Times,* June 26, 1940.

105. *Ibid.*

106. Estimate Proceedings, June 28, 1940.

107. There was one further skirmish over the Planning Commission's proposal. City Councilman Joseph E. Kinsley (Democrat, Bronx) introduced a bill on July 2, 1940, to curtail the Planning Commission's powers by requiring a two-thirds *approval* from the Board of Estimate for zoning amendments (instead of a three-quarters *veto* to block an amendment). The bill passed the council in a straight party vote, the Democrats versus the Fusionists and Reformers. It never came to a vote on the Board of Estimate, however. The New York *Times* (July 30, 1940) credited the Twenty-third Street Association with the original initiative on the bill. Tugwell ("Implementing the General Interest") thought it was the "real estate interests" working with the borough presidents, especially Lyons of the Bronx. There was only limited support for the bill, and the Citizens Union and the City Club opposed it vigorously.

108. The Tugwell master plan was a source of conflict in its own right. It was never completed, although a full land use plan was presented. The plan was most controversial in its treatment of Manhattan commercial and residential districts, for which the plan proposed a "Garden City" concept. This would have entailed taking large segments of the city out of economic use. It is not suprising that the plan was greeted with skepticism and anger. See the New York *Times,* December 13, 14, 15, 20, 1940; April 27, June 5, 19, 1941; January 5, February 11, 12, 1942.

109. *Ibid.,* July 26, 1941.

110. Salmon and Moses were not actually sworn in until January 1, 1942.

111. Moses had said of the Tugwell master plan, "This represents the kind of ivory tower, theoretical planning which dresses up revolutionary ideas." New York *Times,* December 12, 1940. When offered an appointment to the original Planning Commission, Moses refused, saying it would be "trading the substance for the shadow." Cleveland Rodgers, *Robert Moses: Builder for Democracy* (New York, Henry Holt and Co., 1952), p. 128.

112. There is no adequate description of Moses' activities or

theories of city planning. Rogers, *Moses,* is a highly laudatory biography of its subject. J. Clarence Davies III, "Neighborhood Groups and the Urban Renewal Process" (Columbia University doctoral dissertation, 1965), has a brief but excellent summary of Moses' career and personality.

113. City Planning Commission, "Report on the Amendment of the Zoning Resolution," 1944.

114. *Ibid.*

115. CPC Minutes, June 14, 1944. Huie, like Moses, held more than one position. He was commissioner of public works at the same time he was on the Planning Commission and was often viewed as an ally of Moses.

116. CPC Minutes, June 28, 1944; New York *Times,* June 29, 1944.

117. CPC Minutes, July 12, 1944. It seems that Moses was the principal mover in the decision to press for almost immediate action on the plan.

118. Briefs and letters filed with the Planning Commission, contained in the CPC Minutes, August 30, 1944. See also New York *Times,* July 26, 30; August 3, 6, 8, 11, 18, 1944.

119. CPC Minutes, August 30, 1944.

120. *Ibid.,* September 13, 1944.

121. *Ibid.*

122. *Ibid.*

123. New York *Times,* September 29, 1944.

124. *Ibid.,* September 30, 1944.

125. A member of the committee recalled in an interview (August 20, 1963): "The basic organizational problem was overcoming the selfishness of [many groups]. That is, it was hard to find a common ground of self-interest on which all could agree. Just bringing them together for a meeting was a difficult task and keeping them together was even more so."

126. The eighteen members included the Commerce and Industry Association, the Murray Hill Association, the New York Building Congress, the Brooklyn and Bronx Chambers of Commerce, the Staten Island Real Estate Board, and the Twenty-third Street Association. The committee also claimed it had made contact with twenty other groups (including the New York Real Estate Board, the New York Chamber of Commerce, and the Broadway Association) which although not ready to join the committee, were sympathetic with its aims. New York *Times,* September 30, 1944.

127. *Ibid.*

128. *Ibid.*

129. *Ibid.*
130. CPC Minutes, October 4, 1944; New York *Times,* October 5, 1944.
131. CPC Minutes, November 1, 1944.
132. New York *Times,* November 12, 1944.
133. The CZC had added the Brooklyn Real Estate Board, the New York Society of Architects, the Building Trades Employees Association, the Citizens Budget Commission, the New York Board of Trade, and the Downtown Brooklyn Association to its rosters by November 15. *Ibid.,* November 16, 1944.
134. *Ibid.,* November 22, 1944.
135. *Ibid.,* November 23, 1944.
136. *Ibid.*
137. 1916 Zoning Resolution, Section Seven.
138. New York *Times,* November 23, 1944.
139. Estimate Proceedings, November 30, 1944.
140. New York *Times,* December 2, 1944.
141. *431 Fifth Avenue Corporation v. City of New York,* 270 New York 241 (1945). The city appealed the decision of the Appellate Division to the Court of Appeals (New York's highest court), which upheld the Appellate Division without an opinion.
142. New York *Times,* July 25, 1945.

Chapter III: Rezoning New York City, 1945–1960

1. For example, between 1934 and 1946 only seven major commercial structures were built in the city. Between 1947 and 1958, ninety-seven were built. New York *Times,* feature article on "City Planning," May 10, 1959.
2. See Appendix A.
3. See Wallace S. Sayre and Herbert Kaufman, *Governing New York City: Politics in the Metropolis* (New York, Russell Sage Foundation, 1960), Chapters VIII–XI, for the role of the bureaucrat in the city's politics. See also Edward C. Banfield and James Q. Wilson, *City Politics* (Cambridge, Mass., Harvard University Press and M. I. T. Press, 1963), pp. 207–23.
4. Warren Moscow, *Politics in the Empire State,* (New York, Alfred A. Knopf, 1948), pp. 97–101. Banfield and Wilson, *City Politics,* pp. 121–24, 145–48.
5. New York *Times,* April 19, 1946; May 8, 1947. A spokesman for the Regional Plan Association commented in the New York *Times,* May 15, 1948, "The City Planning Commission has grad-

ually been diminishing in prestige," and pointed out the need for major zoning revision.

6. *Ibid.,* October 25, 1947. Salmon officially resigned as chairman in November, 1947, to return to his primary interest, institutional architecture.

7. *Ibid.*

8. *Ibid.,* January 14, 1948.

9. *Ibid.*

10. Estimate Proceedings, April 8, 1948. The appropriation requested was for $165,000.

11. New York *Times,* April 9, 1948.

12. *Ibid.,* and May 14, 1948. Cleveland Rodgers, "Reminiscences," Columbia University Oral History Collection, p. 207.

13. New York *Times,* May 14, 1948.

14. *Ibid.,* November 11, 1948.

15. *Ibid.,* September 22, October 7, 1949.

16. Materials on Jerry Finkelstein have been drawn from the files of Theodore Lowi who generously made them available. See Theodore Lowi, *At the Pleasure of the Mayor: Patronage and Power in New York City, 1898–1958* (New York, Free Press of Glencoe, 1964).

17. Finklestein requested staff increases from 66 staff members to 202, and program fund increases from $382,205 to 922,469. New York *Times,* February 2, 1950.

18. *Ibid.*

19. Moses opposed the increases, arguing the Planning Commission had done nothing to deserve or need additional money. Cleveland Rodgers, *Robert Moses: Builder for Democracy* (New York, Henry Holt and Co., 1952), p. 136. The Citizens Union, the Citizens Budget Commission, and the Regional Plan Association all felt that Finkelstein's requests were too high but that the Planning Commission should have more funds and staff. New York *Times,* February 9, 17, 20; March 6, 27, 1950.

20. New York *Times,* May 9, 1950.

21. *Ibid.,* August 8, 1950.

22. *Ibid.,* August 16, 1950.

23. For a fuller description of the 1950 elections, see Charles Garrett, *The La Guardia Years: Machine and Reform Politics in New York City* (New Brunswick, Rutgers University Press, 1961), pp. 319–20.

24. Rodgers, *Moses,* p. 137. Impellitteri had this option since Wagner had been appointed to fill Salmon's unexpired term, and

Finkelstein was appointed to fill what was in effect the rest of Salmon's term of office. Thus when Finkelstein came to office he had only a year to serve until the mayor could decide whether to reappoint him.

25. New York *Times,* October 5, 21, 1950. Under the terms of the HB&A contract, the consultants were required to furnish only one copy of the plan. Impellitteri seemed to believe that Finkelstein would use the plan as a campaign issue in some manner unfavorable to the acting mayor.

26. Estimate Proceedings, October 26, 1950.

27. Information on Bennett is drawn from Lowi, *At the Pleasure of the Mayor.*

28. Harrison, Ballard, and Allen, *Plan for Rezoning New York City: A Report to the New York City Planning Commission* (New York, 1950).

29. New York Chapter of the American Institute of Architects, Committee on Zoning, "Report on the Proposal to Rezone New York City," May 1, 1951.

30. Citizens Union, Subcommittee on Zoning, "Report on the Proposal to Rezone New York City," November, 1951.

31. New York *Times,* December 31, 1951.

32. Moses appears to have had no objection to this activity, perhaps because he was confident it would lead to no result.

33. CPC Minutes, March 5, 1952.

34. Metropolitan Real Estate Boards Association, *A Critical Analysis of the Plan for Rezoning New York City,* June, 1952.

35. If transcripts were taken of the HB&A hearings, research failed to uncover them. The following description of the hearings is drawn from CPC Minutes and the New York *Times* (appropriate dates).

36. Hearings were held on March 25 and 31; April 8, 18, and 22, 1952.

37. MREBA, *Critical Analysis.*

38. The members of the committee were: Henry J. Davenport, New York Real Estate Board (chairman); Frank A. Barrera, Brooklyn Real Estate Board; Alfred N. Warwick, Long Island (Queens) Real Estate Board; Leonard V. Lavelle, Bronx Real Estate Board; Carl F. Ettlinger, Staten Island Real Estate Board. *Ibid.*

39. *Ibid.*

40. By 1947 the CZC membership had dropped from fifty-one members (in 1944) to thirty-three. Apparently many of those remaining as "members" simply had not bothered to withdraw formally, and it seems that the CZC held few if any meetings in the

period 1947 to 1952. New York *Times,* November 18, 1947; December 18, 1952.

41. *Ibid.,* November 8, 1952.

42. *Ibid.,* December 17, 1952. The CZC apparently never achieved the multi-interest base it had had during the 1944–45 struggle, remaining primarily a "letterhead" group representing the real estate boards.

43. *Ibid.,* December 20, 1952.

44. The Broadway Association, for example, endorsed the plan because it feared that the Times Square area was becoming a "honky-tonk" district and the association believed more restrictive zoning would protect the area.

45. While it is now impossible to say whether all the groups opposing the HB&A proposal ever achieved any unity of action, it does seem clear that the Squire report served as a source for cues and presented a common rallying point for opposition to the proposal.

46. The Master Planning Section had its headquarters in Brooklyn and was not moved to Manhattan until late in 1953. It then occupied space several blocks from the commission offices. The remaining staff members were split among a number of floors and offices in the quarters they occupied.

47. New York *Times,* August 14, 1953.

48. *Ibid.*

49. To limit the "Wagner Era" to 1953–60 is not quite accurate. At the time of writing (fall, 1964) the mayor was still in office.

50. John McDonald, "The $2-Billion Building Boom," *Fortune Magazine,* February, 1960.

51. See Appendix A.

52. James Q. Wilson, *The Amateur Democrat: Club Politics in Three Cities* (Chicago, University of Chicago Press, 1962), especially pp. 37–39.

53. It may be years before anyone can say whether Wagner was "Reformer" or "Regular." He came through the party ranks like a Regular and many of the characteristics of his political manner smacked of "old style" politics. On the other hand, Wagner frequently behaved like a Reformer and his personal commitments seemed to be those of a Reform-oriented politician. This ambiguity, of course, may be part of the secret of Wagner's success.

54. Banfield and Wilson, *City Politics,* Chapter 11, gives a vivid and penetrating analysis of the Reform ideology and program and offers comparisons between the earlier Reform movements and the Reform Democrats.

55. Materials on James Felt have been drawn from Lowi, *At the Pleasure of the Mayor.*

56. New York *Times,* February 12, 1956.

57. By 1960 the staff had grown from barely 100 members to 180, appropriations had increased by roughly a third, and the commission and staff were housed in new and spacious offices. Felt's build-up of the commission can be followed in the City Planning Commission *Newsletter,* published irregularly.

58. New York *Times,* July 23, 1956.

59. Estimate Proceedings, August 30, 1956. Robert Moses sent a letter to the board saying, "There are plenty of worthy, limited objectives to pursue without heading straight for the millennium." New York *Times,* August 31, 1956.

60. For a thorough analysis of the process of formulating the plan, see Frances Piven, "Function of Research in the Formation of City Planning Policy" (University of Chicago doctoral dissertation, 1962).

61. The planners apparently also considered the possibility that Mayor Wagner might be defeated in 1961 and that his successor could be less sympathetic to comprehensive zoning. Another factor may well have been that the planners were anxious to keep zoning from being a campaign issue, to "keep planning out of politics."

62. The proposed performance standards were methods of limiting the amount of noise, fumes, noxious odors, and other "objectionable" features of industrial activity.

63. Ridgewood *Times,* February 15, 1959; New York *Times,* March 2, 1959.

64. New York *Times,* March 2, 1959.

65. *Ibid.,* February 17, 1959.

66. *Ibid.,* February 20, 1959; Long Island *Daily Advocate,* February 20, 1959. Clancy was attempting to walk the line between the claims of the homeowners and those of the local business groups. The homeowners' groups felt that the BSA had been too free in granting variances allowing retail activities to encroach on residential areas; local business groups tended to support the BSA.

67. New York *Times,* February 23, 1959.

68. *Ibid.*

69. *Ibid.,* March 6, 1959.

70. *Ibid.,* March 9, 1959.

71. New York *World Telegram and Sun,* March 19, April 3, 1959; New York *Times,* February 22, April 7 and 12, 1959.

72. New York *Times,* March 30, 1959.

73. This dissatisfaction was expressed by a number of Reform groups and members of the Planning Commission staff. One respondent said; "If the proposal was sound, if it was in the best interests of the city, then what justification could there be for delaying enforcement?" This same respondent went on to admit that perhaps it was necessary and expedient to make the concession, but that perhaps it was granted "too early."

74. New York *Times,* April 13, 1959. Hulan Jack's opposition appears to have been based on two factors: first, the borough president's sincere belief that the proposal was aimed to discriminate against Negroes, a belief that careful examination of the proposal does not bear out in fact; and second, the familiar fear that the Planning Commission was usurping the functions of the borough presidents.

75. *Ibid.*

76. The following account of the informal public hearings is drawn from the unofficial notes taken by Mrs. Frances Piven and the quasi-official *Record of the Informal Hearings* kept by the Planning Commission, City-Wide Hearings, April 13 and 14, 1959; Bronx Hearings, April 27, 1959; Queens Hearings, May 5, 1959; Staten Island Hearings, May 7, 1959; Manhattan Hearings, May 11, 1959; and Brooklyn Hearings, May 11, 1959.

77. These groups were the Metropolitan Outdoor Advertising Association, the Petroleum Association, and a few local garage organizations.

78. Bronx Informal Hearings, April 27, 1959. The informal hearings abound with requests by Felt to "come and see us" and statements that "we're not sure about" this provision or that.

79. For the formation of these alliances, see the Brooklyn, Bronx, and Staten Island informal hearings.

80. New York *Times,* May 7, 1959; Planning Commission, *Newsletter,* May, 1959.

81. Robert Dowling as quoted in the New York *Times,* May 7, 1959.

82. New York *Times,* May 11, 1959.

83. *Ibid.,* June 24, 1959.

84. *Ibid.,* June 28, 1959.

85. Metropolitan Real Estate Boards Association, *Analysis with Respect to the Proposed Comprehensive Amendment to the Zoning Resolution,* November, 1959.

86. New York *Times,* December 1, 1959.

87. *Ibid.*

88. *Ibid.,* December 2, 1959.

89. Specifically, Madison, Park, Lexington, and Third avenues. City Planning Commission, "Revision of the Voorhees, Walker, Smith and Smith Plan for Rezoning New York City," December, 1959.

90. New York *Herald Tribune,* December 12, 1959.

91. *Ibid.*

92. New York *Times,* December 12, 1959.

93. As an example, Felt had two members of the staff working with the City Island Civic Association for months. The public hearings show a touching devotion and gratitude toward Felt from this group.

94. New York *Times,* February 12, 1960.

95. New York *Journal-American,* February 15, 1960.

96. City Planning Commission, *Transcript of the Public Hearings,* March 14, 1960.

97. *Ibid.*

98. *Ibid.*

99. *Ibid.*

100. *Ibid.*

101. In Staten Island, for example, the Staten Island Chamber of Commerce, Real Estate Board, Chapter of the AIA, and Home Builders Association were in opposition. The Staten Island Civic Congress (a federated homeowners' association) strongly favored the code.

102. The borough hearings were held as follows: in the Bronx, March 18, 1960; Brooklyn, March 21, 1960; Manhattan, March 22, 1960; Queens, March 23, 1960; Staten Island, March 25, 1960.

103. Feelings were exacerbated by events occuring within the boroughs. For example, on March 21, the Queens Chamber of Commerce invited a number of homeowners' groups to a meeting to oppose the proposal. The Federation of Queens Civic Councils shunned the meeting, and when the Chamber of Commerce announced that it had the homeowners on its side, the lines of division between the two groups were sharpened. See the Long Island *Press and Star Journal,* March 22, 1960. Queens Hearings, *Transcript.*

104. As read into the March 25, 1960, *transcript* of the hearings.

105. City Club, "Comments," April 8, 1960.

106. New York *Times,* June 7, 1960.

107. *Ibid.,* June 8, 1960.

108. See correspondence to the City Planning Commission from Robert Moses, dated November 6, 1957; September 13, 1960; December 13, 1960; in the files of the City Planning Commission.

109. City Planning Commission, "List of Changes in the Final Draft of the Proposed Comprehensive Amendment to the Zoning Resolution," August 17, 1960.

110. New York *Times,* September 8, 1960.

111. *Ibid.,* September 9, 1960.

112. *Ibid.,* September 10, 1960.

113. *Ibid.,* January 14, 1960.

114. CPC Minutes, October 18, 1960.

115. Estimate Proceedings, November 21, 22, 1960.

116. Estimate Proceedings, December 15, 1960. According to one story, Bronx Borough President Lyons had decided to vote against the proposal, "grass-roots support" for the proposal notwithstanding. The mayor is supposed to have brought last-minute pressure to bear to change Lyons' mind. It is worth noting that Lyons was the only member of the Board of Estimate who did not make a statement at the meeting praising the Planning Commission. The Bronx borough president preferred to remain silent.

Chapter IV: The Governmental Participants and the Rules of the Game

1. See Chapter VI for the "short-run" factors.

2. Wallace S. Sayre and Herbert Kaufman, *Governing New York City: Politics in the Metropolis* (New York, Russell Sage Foundation, 1960), p. 92.

3. *Ibid.*

4. *Ibid.,* pp. 105–8, points out that one political strategy is to attempt to win changes in the rules favorable to an actor's interests.

5. *Ibid.,* p. 92.

6. New York City Charter (1901) as amended by Laws of 1914, Chapter 470, Sections 242a and 242b.

7. Sayre and Kaufman, *Governing New York City,* Chapter XVII, especially p. 626.

8. During the period 1917–32, split votes on zoning questions in the Board of Estimate were rare—a result of the "cult of unanimity" that led the board to try to present a united front to the public. *Ibid.,* p. 640. An examination of thirty-seven votes on zoning questions showed the borough presidents consistently voting as a bloc. There were, however, only five split votes.

9. John P. Comer, *New York City Building Control, 1800–1941* (New York: Columbia University Press, 1942), Chapter 4.

10. Actually the Board of Standards and Appeals went through two major reorganizations during the period under consideration.

Originally the building superintendents had a place on the board, but as members of the BSA were not allowed to consider zoning questions. In 1925 the BSA was reorganized, its membership reduced, and all the members but one appointed by the mayor. In 1935 the BSA was once again reorganized, reduced in size, and all but one out of the four members appointed by the mayor. See Joseph D. McGoldrick, Seymour Graubard, and Raymond J. Horowitz, *Building Regulation in New York City* (New York, Commonwealth Fund, 1944), pp. 104–6.

11. Comer, *New York City Building Control,* Chapter 4.

12. This was changed in 1958 to four votes each for the city-wide officers and two votes each for the borough presidents—a total of twenty-two votes with sixteen representing a three-quarters veto. The combination of votes needed to block a proposal did not change, however.

13. See New York City Charter (1938), Chapter 8, for the formal description of the process of passing a zoning amendment.

14. The Board of Aldermen was replaced by a smaller City Council in the 1938 Charter. The council was intended to be more powerful than the Board of Aldermen, but this did not prove to be the case. Sayre and Kaufman, *Governing New York City,* pp. 609–11.

15. New York City Charter (1938), Chapter 8, describes the formal composition and powers of the City Planning Commission.

16. See Sayre and Kaufman, *Governing New York City,* pp. 632–39, for a description of the place of each of the Board of Estimate's members in the city bureaucracy.

17. *Ibid.,* pp. 73–74. The major exception was the Planning Commission.

18. *Ibid.,* pp. 67–70 and 122–41, describes in detail the city's structure and activities.

19. New York *Times,* March 12, March 23, 1929; June 25, June 26, July 8, July 9, 1930.

20. Testimony of C. U. Powell, Queens borough engineer, Charter Commission *Records* (April 24, 1935); testimony of J. A. Palma, Staten Island borough president, *ibid.* (April 23, 1935); testimony of Vernon S. Moon, chief engineer of the Board of Estimate, *ibid.*

21. La Guardia's indifference toward the Planning Commission increased as the commission consistently failed in its Charter areas.

22. Harvey was borough president of Queens before the La Guardia Fusion organization came into being. He served as borough president from 1929 to 1941, basing his strength primarily on Regular Republican votes.

23. Comer, *New York City Building Control,* pp. 153–54.

24. New York City Charter (1901) as amended in 1916, Section 242; Local Law (1925) No. 13; Local Law (1934) No. 28.

25. Comer, *New York City Building Control,* pp. 138–39, 153–54, and *passim.*

26. *Ibid.* New York *Times,* July 25, 1926; February 21, 1927; October 9, 10, 22, 23, 1929; February 4, 1930; March 5, 1931.

27. Theodore Lowi, *At the Pleasure of the Mayor: Patronage and Power in New York City, 1898–1958* (New York, Free Press of Glencoe, 1964), Chapter 8.

28. James Q. Wilson, *The Amateur Democrat: Club Politics in Three Cities* (Chicago, University of Chicago Press, 1962), pp. 37–39.

29. Sayre and Kaufman, *Governing New York City,* p. 638.

30. The New York *Times,* for example, listed comprehensive zoning as one of Wagner's outstanding achievements. See the issue of April 10, 1963.

31. See Charles S. Ascher, "City Planning, Administration—and Politics," *Land Economics,* Vol. XXX (November, 1954).

32. The borough presidents, the Department of Buildings, and apparently the Department of Parks accused the Planning Commission of raiding their respective staffs for personnel and of attempting to encroach on their jurisdictions. New York *Times,* August 19, 1938.

33. From 1939 to 1950, the commission had a staff of sixty-six members.

34. Mayor's Committee on Management Survey, *Modern Management for the City of New York* (1953), II, 104.

35. New York *Times,* December 1, 1932; March 24, 1935; January 25, 1936.

36. *Ibid.* See also *ibid.,* June 6, July 16, November 7, 1956; January 17, 18, February 2, 15, 1957.

37. Sayre and Kaufman, *Governing New York City,* pp. 270–71.

38. See *ibid.,* Chapter XIV, for a description of the New York City courts and the politics of the judicial process. See also McGoldrick and others, *Building Regulation,* Chapters IV, V, VII, IX, and X, for a detailed discussion of the role of the courts in the zoning process.

39. For a description of these agencies, see Sayre and Kaufman, *Governing New York City:* for the Department of Parks, pp. 379–80; for the Department of Traffic, pp. 295–98; for the Port of New York Authority, pp. 321–22.

Chapter V: The Nongovernmental Participants

1. Sidney Verba, *Small Groups and Political Behavior* (Princeton, Princeton University Press, 1961), pp. 153–54, 185–92.

2. The major written sources for the building groups were: John P. Comer, *New York City Building Control, 1800–1941* (New York, Columbia University Press, 1942); Building Trades Employers Association, *Handbook; The Real Estate Record and Guide;* testimony of group representatives at public hearings.

3. Planning Commission, *Record of the Informal Hearings,* May 19, 1959.

4. Planning Commission, *Transcript of the Public Hearings,* March 14, 1960.

5. Appendix B suggests some of the differences among the boroughs in population growth and densities.

6. New York *Times,* May 3, 1914.

7. *Ibid.,* July 26, August 18, 1944.

8. During an interview with the author a spokesman for a labor union said, "We follow zoning policy, of course, but it rarely affects what the building trades employee is doing." See, however, New York *Times,* July 18, 1963, in which the Building and Construction Trades Council (an association of 122 unions) expressed fears over the effects of the 1960 Zoning Resolution.

9. Major sources on the architectural groups were: American Institute of Architects, *Directory;* New York Chapter of the AIA, *Report* on the 1959 zoning proposal; Planning Commission, *Transcript.*

10. The Metropolitan Real Estate Boards Association relied heavily on the advice of an architect during the 1949 and 1959–60 controversies. And, in both cases, the consultants to the Planning Commission were architectural firms.

11. There are also two parallel groups: the New York (Manhattan) Society of Architects and the Brooklyn Society of Architects. The Architectural League of New York, a city-wide organization, was more concerned with civic art and aesthetics than with the practical problems of zoning policy.

12. Major sources for the discussion of the real estate community were: the respective *Annual Diaries* of the real estate boards of New York, Long Island, Brooklyn, and the Bronx; *The Real Estate Record and Guide;* New York Real Estate Board, *Newsletter;* MREBA, *Reports,* 1950 and 1959; *Realty Facts,* a monthly bulletin of the Brooklyn Real Estate Board, June, 1947, to June, 1951; *The Real Estate News,* 1956 to 1961; *The Real Estate and Building Management Digest,* April-May, 1914, and February, 1915; the New

York *Times,* especially April 17, 1914, for a history of the New York Real Estate Board to that time; the statements of the representatives of the real estate groups at the public hearings.

13. Obviously many realtors may be engaged in both types of activity. But there is a tendancy toward specialization, recognized to the extent that the New York Real Estate Board, for example, has separate "Owners" and "Managers" and "Brokerage" divisions.

14. Lawrence McGuire, president of the New York Real Estate Board (1914 to 1918), as quoted in the New York *Times,* January 18, 1914.

15. New York *Times,* June 11, 1927. The membership of the five real estate boards in 1962 in round numbers was: New York Real Estate Board: 3,050; Long Island (including members from Nassau and Suffolk counties): 2,000; Brooklyn: 700; Bronx: 410; Staten Island: 150.

16. Statement of I. I. Rosenbaum, *Transcript,* March 14, 1960.

17. See, e.g., the statement of Frank Barrera, *ibid.*

18. Major sources for the description of the general business groups were: Joseph B. Bishop, *Chronicle of 150 Years: The Chamber of Commerce of the State of New York, 1768 to 1918* (New York, Charles Scribner's Sons, 1918); Commerce and Industry Association, *Bulletin,* 1941–45, 1949–53; Citizens Budget Commission, *Citizens in Action* (New York, 1960); Citizens Budget Commission, *Sentinel* (Special Edition), January 9, 1957.

For the local business groups: Chamber of Commerce of the Borough of Queens *Queensborough,* Vol. I (May, 1914) through Vol. XXXIII (December, 1957); Fifth Avenue Association, *Annual Reports,* especially 1907 to 1916 and 1940 to 1960; Fifth Avenue Association, *Fifty Years on Fifth* (New York, 1957); testimony of various groups' representatives, 1915, 1916, and *Transcript,* March and September, 1960.

19. Informal Hearings Report, April 13, 1959. See also the May 19, 1959, hearings when the Executive Director of the Citizens Budget Commission said: "Nothing can do more for the city than a program for growth and insurance against an economic decline. . . . But what should be in the ordinance? Men of good will will find ways to agree insofar as industry and the rest of the community is concerned. Brooklyn civic leaders should and must come forward with their suggestions."

20. New York *Times,* March 24, 1924; March 25, 1930; November 25, 1935; June 26, 1936; January 10, 1938.

21. *Transcript,* September 12, 1960.

22. Informal Hearings Report, May 19, 1959.

23. The names of these groups can be misleading. The Fifth Avenue Association, for example, did not confine its jurisdiction to Fifth Avenue alone, but included part of Madison Avenue, Park Avenue, and the cross streets.

24. See the Fifth Avenue Association, *Annual Reports,* e.g., 1912 to 1916.

25. There are few written sources on these groups in New York City. J. Clarence Davies III, "Neighborhood Groups and the Urban Renewal Process" (Columbia University doctoral dissertation, 1965), covers a number of Manhattan and Queens groups. See also Caroline Ware, *Greenwich Village: 1920–1930* (Boston, Houghton Mifflin, 1935), especially Chapter IV.

26. *Transcript,* September 13, 1960.

27. Informal Hearings Report, April 14, 1959.

28. The nomenclature of these groups is frequently confusing. Many "civic associations" are purely homeowners' groups.

29. The counsel and president of several of these groups stressed this distinction between the two types of groups in a personal interview with the author.

30. Informal Hearings Report, May 19, 1959.

31. The major written sources for these groups were: Wallace S. Sayre and Herbert Kaufman, *Governing New York City: Politics in the Metropolis* (New York, Russell Sage Foundation, 1960), pp. 497–502; Henry J. Curran, *Pillar to Post* (New York, Charles Scribner's Sons, 1941); Regional Plan Association, *Annual Reports,* 1938–42, 1948–54; Forbes B. Hays, *Community Leadership: The Regional Plan Association of New York* (New York, Columbia University Press, 1965); Citizens Union, "Report on the Proposed Comprehensive Amendment to the Zoning Resolution." 1960.

George McAneny, "Reminiscences," Columbia University Oral History Collection, pp. 5–7 and *passim,* has references to the early histories of the City Club, the Citizens Union, and the Regional Plan Association—all organizations with which McAneny had a more than passing acquaintance.

32. See, for example, Citizens Union, "Report," 1960.

33. Sources for the discussion of the press were: Sayre and Kaufman, *Governing New York City,* pp. 81–86, and the files of the papers themselves.

34. There are limits on the availability of staff for a particular issue, however. The larger and more diversified the interest group, even though its staff may be proportionately larger, the more staff time is taken with organization maintenance and dealing with a wide range of activities. As one participant (a local business group

leader) said: "Our staff is small—less than seven. The Commerce and Industry Association, for example, has upwards of eighty. But look at the difference. We concentrate on only a relatively small area, while they are trying to cover the whole city or more. And no one can say who really has the staffing advantage."

35. The leader of one interest group was described as "too old to throw out, too conservative to be moved, too sure to listen." Another was criticized as follows: "If he had been capable of listening, of negotiating [in 1959 and 1960], he could have gotten a lot more for us than he did. As it was he and [his organization] did not get anything."

36. In fact, research has failed to uncover any overt efforts to impose sanctions on dissenting groups. Although on occasion disgruntlement and bitterness ran high, one of the informal rules of the nongovernmental actors appears to have been the acceptance (in public, at least) of the autonomy of each group.

37. There are no entirely satisfactory studies of these multiple memberships available. The research probelms posed by any thoroughgoing study and analysis are formidable, involving not only the sociometry of multiple memberships but the meaningfulness of these memberships to the holders and to the political process. David B. Truman, *The Governmental Process: Political Interests and Public Opinion* (New York, Alfred A. Knopf, 1960), p. 168 and *passim,* lays out a careful consideration of the possible effects of overlapping memberships on interest group behavior.

38. These groups were the Fifty-seventh Street Association, the Madison Avenue Association, the Park Avenue South Association, and the Midtown Association.

39. In 1916, e.g., Walter Stabler, one of the members of the Zoning Commission, was on the Executive Committee of the Fifth Avenue Association and was a past vice-president of the New York Real Estate Board.

40. See Informal Hearings Report, May 19, 1959.

41. An additional element is that groups may share the same legal or public relations consultant without the groups sharing any congruence of interests.

42. This is also ruefully admitted by their opponents.

43. Or so many group leaders claim.

Chapter VI: Processes and Strategies

1. Although this is generally true, there were exceptions. The labor unions were occasionally participants (see Chapter V); a few

organized tenant groups appeared, although intermittently. The Urban League acted as spokesman for the Negro in the 1959–60 controversy, but its role was almost entirely symbolic. It spoke at one of the hearings in general support of the Planning Commission's proposal and allowed the matter to rest there. Hulan Jack saw himself in part as representing the interests of the Negro in Harlem, although this stand was inextricably tied to the problem of the borough president's autonomy.

2. It should be noted that, according to the U.S. Census of Housing for 1960, there were 577,012 owner-occpuied housing units in the city; there were 2,077,890 rented-occupied units. Over 50 percent (289,428) of the owner-occupied dwelling units were occupied by a single family.

The median income of those owning their own home was $7,000 a year; of those renting their homes, $5,000 a year.

3. It is also possible that some groups who did not have a major commitment to the issues simply did not bother to exert themselves beyond a few symbolic gestures.

4. As a contrast, the author was interviewing one of the staff executives of a prestigious Manhattan interest group when the latter was interrupted by phone calls to the extent of three or four in an hour by various city government officials who wanted to try out ideas on the group staff member. He, in his turn, chatted with officials in a familiar (often first-name basis) and comfortable manner. A group so happily placed has an inside tract on information and can plan its actions far in advance of its less well-informed fellow organizations. Such a group also had a far better opportunity to have a voice in the early stages of policy formulation.

5. This argument is drawn from the data presented in Chapter II and from inferences from the New York *Times* and interviews. It seems that the borough presidents' office and the party organizations felt quite strongly that open conflicts should be avoided whenever possible.

6. The hypothesis that conflicts became increasingly public and governmental is based on a survey of the New York *Times* from 1916 to 1960. Of course, the press reports only public conflicts and the coverage may often depend on the other news available. Moreover, such factors as fluctuations in the real estate market, the increasing number of active interest groups, and increasing population (and hence greater pressures on the same amount of land) might all be equally operable. This hypothesis was, however, suggested by interviewees who had seen both systems in operation.

See also E. E. Schattschneider, "Intensity, Visibility, Direction, and Scope," *American Political Science Review,* LI (1957), 953–54: "The important point about pressure politics is not that it is a conflict of private interests, but the fact that private politics are taken into the public domain. Pressure politics is therefore a stage in the socialization of conflict; it represents the breakdown of the attempt to privatize conflict."

7. Wallace S. Sayre and Herbert Kaufman, *Governing New York City: Politics in the Metropolis* (New York, Russell Sage Foundation, 1960), Chapter XIII.

8. This description of the bargaining process was suggested in part by Thomas C. Schelling, "An Essay on Bargaining," in Nelson W. Polsby, Robert A. Dentler, Paul A. Smith, eds., *Politics and Social Life* (Boston, Houghton Mifflin Company, 1963), pp. 416–32.

Chapter VII: The Politics of Zoning

1. Paul A. Preftzschner, "Planning—City to Nation," *National Civic Review,* L, No. 8 (September, 1961), 419.

2. The concept of the "public interest" is a knotty puzzle of conflicting and divergent viewpoints. For a recent attempt to clarify some of the mysteries attached to the idea of the public interest, see Carl J. Friedrich, ed., *The Public Interest* (New York, Atherton Press, 1962). See also Martin Meyerson and Edward C. Banfield, *Politics, Planning, and the Public Interest* (New York, Free Press of Glencoe, 1955), Chapter 11.

3. See Frances Piven, "Function of Research in the Formation of City Planning Policy" (University of Chicago doctoral dissertation, 1962), for a study of the conflicts among goals and methods for planners in arriving at the public interest.

4. See William Alonso, "Cities and City Planners," *Daedalus,* Vol. XCII, No. 4 (Fall, 1963), especially pp. 828–29, for a statement of this aspect of planning and zoning.

5. Wallace S. Sayre and Herbert Kaufman, *Governing New York City: Politics in the Metropolis* (New York, Russell Sage Foundation, 1960), p. 722.

6. Obviously, zoning also provided a process for the settlement of conflicts that arose in the "private sphere" of the city.

7. Sayre and Kaufman, *Governing New York City,* pp. 712–13.

8. *Ibid.,* p. 715.

9. *Ibid.,* p. 710.

10. *Ibid.* p. 716.

11. Sayre and Kaufman suggest this fact themselves. *Ibid.,* p. 713.

12. William H. Form and Delbert C. Miller, *Industry, Labor, and Community* (New York, Harper and Brothers, 1960), p. 160.

13. Oliver P. Williams and Charles R. Adrian, *Four Cities: A Study in Comparative Policy Making* (Philadelphia, University of Pennsylvania Press, 1963).

14. Sidney M. Wilhelm, *Urban Zoning and Land Use Theory* (New York, Free Press of Glencoe, 1962), after an intensive study of the ecological forces guiding zoning in Austin, Texas, argues this viewpoint.

15. Robert C. Wood suggests this in *1400 Governments: The Political Economy of the New York Metropolitan Region* (Cambridge, Mass. Harvard University Press, 1961), especially Chapter 3.

16. Harold Kaplan, *Urban Renewal Politics: Slum Clearance in Newark* (New York, Columbia University Press, 1963).

17. *Ibid.,* p. 170.

18. Peter H. Rossi and Robert A. Dentler, *The Politics of Urban Renewal: The Chicago Findings* (New York, Free Press of Glencoe, 1961), especially Chapter 6.

19. *Ibid.,* Chapter 7.

20. Robert A. Dahl, *Who Governs? Democracy and Power in an American City* (New Haven, Yale University Press, 1961).

21. *Ibid.,* Chapter 10 and 11.

22. Matthew Holren, Jr., "The Governance of the Metropolis as a Probelm in Diplomacy," *Journal of Politics,* Vol. XXVI, No. 3 (August, 1964).

23. See, for example, Jane Jacobs, *The Death and Life of Great American Cities* (New York, Random House, 1961), for one of the most outstanding critics of urban renewal.

24. New York City, in 1961, adopted a new City Charter that placed the Planning Commission directly under the mayor, ostensibly to strengthen the Planning Commission.

25. Robert Walker, *The Planning Function in Urban Government* (Chicago, University of Chicago Press, 1950), has been one of the most prominent advocates of this structural reform. For a dissenting view, see T. J. Kent, Jr., *The Urban General Plan* (San Francisco, Chandler Publishing Company, 1964).

SELECTED BIBLIOGRAPHY

Alonso, William. "Cities and City Planners," *Daedalus*, Vol. XCII, No. 4 (Fall, 1963).

Amberg, Edna, and William H. Allen. Civic Lessons from Mayor Mitchel's Defeat. New York, Institute for Public Service, 1921.

Ascher, Charles S. "City Planning, Administration—and Politics," *Land Economics*, Vol. XXX, No. 4 (November, 1954).

Banfield, Edward C. Political Influence. New York, Free Press of Glencoe, 1961.

Banfield, Edward C., and James Q. Wilson. City Politics. Cambridge, Mass., Harvard University Press and M.I.T. Press, 1963.

Bassett, Edward M. Autobiography. New York; Harbor Press, 1939. Zoning: The Laws, Administration, and Court Decisions During the First Twenty Years. New York, Russell Sage Foundation, 1936.

Beshers, J. N. Urban Social Structure. New York, Free Press of Glencoe, 1962.

Black, Russel Van Nest. "The Planning Profession's Responsibility to the People," *Journal of the American Institute of Planners*, Vol. XIV, No. 4 (948).

Burck, Gilbert. "Headquarters Town," *Fortune Magazine*, February, 1960.

Chamber of Commerce of New York State. "A Modern Zoning Resolution for the City of New York." New York, 1959.

Chamber of Commerce of the United States. "Zoning: A Statement of Principles and Practices." Washington, D.C., 1929.

Chapin, F. Stuart, Jr. Urban Land Use Planning. New York, Harper and Brothers, 1957.

Chicago Real Estate Board. Studies on Building Height Limitations in Large Cities. Chicago, 1923.

Citizens Budget Commission. Citizens in Action: The Citizens Budget Commission Story. New York, 1960.

Citizens Housing and Planning Council. Citizens Guide to Zoning. New York, 1959.

Citizens Union. "Report on the Proposal to Rezone New York City." New York, 1951.

——. "Report on the Proposed Amendment to the Zoning Resolution." New York, 1960.

Comer, John P. New York City Building Control, 1800–1941. New York, Columbia University Press, 1942.

Committee for Modern Zoning. A City Speaks. Englewood Cliffs, N.J., Prentice-Hall, 1960.

Dahl, Robert A. Who Governs? Democracy and Power in an American City. New Haven, Yale University Press, 1961.

Dahl, Robert A., and Edward Lindbloom. Politics, Economics, and Welfare. New York, Harper and Brothers, 1953.

Davies, J. Clarence, III. "Neighborhood Groups and the Urban Renewal Process." Columbia University doctoral dissertation, 1965.

Duhl, Leonard, ed. The Urban Condition: People and Policy in the Metropolis. New York, Basic Books, 1964.

Ehrmann, Henry W., ed. Interest Groups on Four Continents. Pittsburgh, University of Pittsburgh Press, 1958.

Fifth Avenue Association. Fifty Years on Fifth: 1907 to 1957. New York, 1957.

Firey, Walter. Land Use in Central Boston. Cambridge, Mass., Harvard University Press, 1947.

Ford, Gordon B. "How New York City Now Controls the Development of Private Property." New York, 1916 (?). Pamphlet on file at Columbia University Avery Library.

Friedrich, Carl J., ed. The Public Interest. New York, Atherton Press, 1962.

Garrett, Charles. The La Guardia Years: Machine and Reform Politics in New York City. New Brunswick, Rutgers University Press, 1961.

Greer, Scott. Governing the Metropolis. New York, John Wiley and Sons, 1962.

Handlin, Oscar. The Newcomers. Cambridge, Mass., Harvard University Press, 1959.

Harrison, Ballard, and Allen. Plan for Rezoning New York City: A Report to the City Planning Commission. New York, 1950.

Hays, Forbes B. Community Leadership: The Regional Plan Association of New York. New York, Columbia University Press, 1963.

Hofstadter, Richard. The Age of Reform: From Bryan to F.D.R. New York, Alfred A. Knopf, 1955.

Hunter, Floyd. Community Power Structure. Chapel Hill, University of North Carolina Press, 1953.

Jacobs, Jane. The Death and Life of Great American Cities. New York, Random House, 1961.

Kaplan, Harold. Urban Renewal Politics: Slum Clearance in Newark. New York, Columbia University Press, 1963.

Leary, Robert M. A Model Procedure for the Administration of Zoning Regulations. Washington, D.C., Urban Land Institute, 1958.

Leiserson, Avery. Administrative Regulation: A Study in Representation of Interests. Chicago, University of Chicago Press, 1942.

Lewinson, Edwin R. "John Purroy Mitchel: Symbol of Reform." Columbia University doctoral dissertation, 1961.

Lowi, Theodore. At the Pleasure of the Mayor: Patronage and Power in New York City, 1898–1958. New York, Free Press of Glencoe, 1964.

Lubove, Roy. The Progressives and the Slums: 1890–1917. Pittsburgh, University of Pittsburgh Press, 1962.

McAneny, George. "Reminiscences." Columbia University Oral History Collection.

McDonald, John. "The $2-Billion Building Boom," Fortune Magazine, February, 1960.

McGoldrick, John D., Seymour Graubard, and Raymond J. Horowitz. Building Regulation in New York City. New York, Commonwealth Fund, 1944.

Metropolitan Real Estate Boards Association. Analysis with Respect to the Proposed Comprehensive Amendment to the Zoning Resolution. New York, 1959.

——. A Critical Analysis of the Plan for Rezoning New York City. New York, 1952.

Meyerson, Martin, and Edward C. Banfield. Politics, Planning, and the Public Interest. New York, Free Press of Glencoe, 1955.

New York City
  Board of Elections. Annual Report. 1936.
  Board of Estimate. Journal of Proceedings. 1934–60.
  Board of Estimate and Apportionment. Minutes. 1911–34.
  Board of Estimate and Apportionment, Commission on Building Districts and Restrictions. Report. June 2, 1916.
  ——. Transcripts of the Public Hearings. March and April, 1916.
  Board of Estimate and Apportionment, Commission on the Height and Arrangement of Buildings. Report. December 13, 1913.
  Board of Estimate and Apportionment, Committee on City Planning. Report. July 18, 1916.
  ——. Transcript of the Public Hearings, January, 1915.

New York City *(Continued)*
    Board of Estimate and Apportionment, Subcommittee on the Relation of the Proposed Plan to Other Plans of City Development. Report. June 15, 1916.
    Board of Estimate and Apportionment, Subcommittee to Consider the Districting Resolution. Report, June 15, 1916.
    Charter. 1901.
    Charter. 1938.
    Charter Revision Commission. Records, Vols. I–XII. 1935–36.
    Mayor's Committee on City Planning and Survey. Report. 1928.
    Mayor's Committee on Management Survey. Modern Management for the City of New York, Volume II. 1953.
    Planning Commission. Annual Report. 1938, 1939, 1940.
    ——. "List of Changes in the Final Draft of the Proposed Comprehensive Amendment to the Zoning Resolution." August, 1960.
    Minutes. 1938–60.
    ——. *Newsletter.* 1956–60.
    ——. Record of the Informal Hearings, 1959.
    ——. "Report on the Amendments of the Zoning Resolution of New York City." 1944.
    ——. "Revision of the Voorhees, Walker, Smith and Smith Plan for Rezoning New York City." December, 1959.
    ——. Transcript of the Public Hearings on the Proposed Amendments to the Zoning Resolution of New York City. March and September, 1960.
    President of the Borough of Manhattan, Fifth Avenue Commission. Report of the Fifth Avenue Commission to the Borough President of Manhattan. 1912.
New York State. Legislative Record and Index. 1929.
Nolting, Orin F., and David S. Arnold, eds. Municipal Year Book, 1960. Chicago, International City Manager's Association, 1960.
Peel, Roy V. Political Clubs of New York. New York, G. P. Putnam's Sons, 1935.
Perloff, Harvey S., ed. Planning and the Urban Community. Pittsburgh, University of Pittsburgh Press, 1961.
Peterson, Lorin. Day of the Mugwump. New York, Random House, 1961.
Piven, Frances. "Function of Research in the Formation of City Planning Policy." University of Chicago doctoral dissertation, 1962.
Preftzschner, Paul A. "Planning—City to Nation," *National Civic Review,* Vol. L, No. 8 (September, 1961).
Purdy, Lawson. "Reminiscences." Columbia University Oral History Collection.

Ratcliff, R. U. Urban Land Economics. New York, McGraw-Hill, 1949.

Rodgers, Cleveland. New York Plans for the Future. New York, Harper and Brothers, 1943.

——. "Reminiscences." Columbia University Oral History Collection.

——. Robert Moses: Builder for Democracy. New York, Henry Holt and Co., 1952.

Rossi, Peter H., and Robert A. Dentler. The Politics of Urban Renewal: The Chicago Findings. New York, Free Press of Glencoe, 1961.

Sayre, Wallace S., and Herbert Kaufman. Governing New York City: Politics in the Metropolis. New York, Russell Sage Foundation, 1960.

Schattschneider, E. E. "Intensity, Visibility, Direction, and Scope," American Political Science Review, Vol. LI (1957).

Shaw, Frederick. History of the New York City Legislature. New York, Columbia University Press, 1954.

Truman, David B. The Governmental Process: Political Interests and Public Opinion. New York, Alfred A. Knopf, 1960.

Tugwell, Rexford G. "The Fourth Power," Planning and Civic Comment, Vol. V (April-June, 1939).

——. "Implementing the General Interest," Public Administration Review, Vol. I, No. 1 (Autumn, 1940).

United States Department of Commerce, Bureau of the Census. Number of Inhabitants: New York State. Washington, D.C., 1960.

Verba, Sidney. Small Groups and Political Behavior. Princeton, Princeton University Press, 1961.

Voorhees, Walker, Smith and Smith. Rezoning New York City. New York, 1959.

Walker, Robert. The Planning Function in Urban Government. Chicago, University of Chicago Press, 1950.

Webster, Donald H. Urban Planning and Municipal Public Policy. New York, Harper and Brothers, 1958.

Weimer, A. M., and H. Hoyt. Principles of Real Estate. New York, Ronald Press, 1954.

Wilhelm, Sidney M. Urban Zoning and Land Use Theory. New York, Free Press of Glencoe, 1962.

Williams, Oliver P., and Charles R. Adrian. Four Cities: A Study in Comparative Policy Making. Philadelphia, University of Pennsylvania Press, 1963.

Wilson, James Q. The Amateur Democrat: Club Politics in Three Cities. Chicago, University of Chicago Press, 1962.

Yokley, E. C. Zoning Law and Practice. Charlottesville, Michie Company, 1953.

INDEX

Administrative agencies, and zoning, 116
Adrian, Charles, *see* Williams, Oliver P.
Advisory Council of Real Estate Interests, council of financial institutions, 32; as a peak association, 139
Allied Realty Interests, 28
American Institute of Architects, 135
Architects, described, 135; divisions among, on zoning, 136–37
Architects Council, 96, 98; described, 135–36; as a peak association, 152
Associated Builders of New York, and zoning, 134
Avenue of Americas Association, 144

Barrera, Frank, 88, 98; opposes Tugwell Plan, 59; offer to compromise on Tugwell Plan, 61; opposes Harrison, Ballard, and Allen Plan, 80; opposition to rezoning, 94; quoted, 100
Bassett, Edward M., 128, 132; described, 9–10; relations with Nelson Lewis and Lawson Purdy, 10; attitude toward subways, 10; chairman of First Zoning Commission, 17; chairman of Second Zoning Commission, 26; efforts to conciliate Fifth Avenue Association, 31; chairman of Subcommittee on Zoning, 45; proposes city planning agency, 46; testimony to Charter Revision Commission, 50; and interest groups, 168; as a Reformer, 183–84
Bennett, John J., appointed chairman of Planning Commission, 75; described, 75; relations with Moses and Impellitteri, 75; and master planning, 75; retires from Planning Commission, 83
Berle, Adolph A., appointed chairman of Planning Commission, 56; and early activities of Planning Commission, 56
Board of Aldermen, creation, 7; *see also* President of the Board of Aldermen
Board of Estimate, 111; creation, 7; empowered to zone, 22–23; hearings on 1916 Zoning Plan, 38; vote on 1916 Zoning Plan, 39–40; and 1916 Zoning Resolution during 1920s, 42; procedure for amending Zoning Resolution during 1920s and 1930s, 42–43; vote on Moses Plan, 68; and Voorhees, Walker, Smith, and Smith Plan, 96–97; hearings on Voorhees, Walker, Smith, and Smith, Plan, 104; described prior to 1938, 111; described after 1938, 113; link with party organizations, 117; uniqueness, 187
Board of Standards and Appeals, 111, 171; relation to zoning during 1920s, 43–44; described prior to 1938, 112; described after 1938, 113; relations with Planning Commission, 114; stake in zoning, 116, 120; relation to party organizations, 120; and interest groups, 120, 127, 162; discussed, 127–28; and courts, 128–29; resources, 131; and the professions, 159